Straight Talk

About Spiritual Stuff

Bil Holton
Cher Holton

Prosperity Publishing House
Durham, NC USA

Copyright ©2012 Bil Holton and Cher Holton

All rights reserved.

Reproduction or translation of any part of this work beyond that permitted by Section 107 or 108 of the 1976 United States Copyright Act without the permission of the copyright owner is unlawful. Requests for permission or further information should be addressed to the authors, c/o Prosperity Publishing House, 1405 Autumn Ridge Drive, Durham. NC 27712.

This publication is designed to provide accurate and authoritative information in regard to the subject matter covered. It is sold with the understanding that the publisher is not engaged in rendering legal, accounting, or other professional service. If legal advice or other expert assistance is required, the services of a competent professional person should be sought. *From a Declaration of Principles jointly adopted by a Committee of the American Bar Association and a Committee of Publishers.*

Prosperity Publishing House
Durham, NC

Library of Congress Cataloging-in-Publication Data

Holton, Bil
Straight Talk About Spiritual Stuff / Bil Holton and Cher Holton
      p. cm.
   Includes bibliographical references.
   ISBN 978-1-893095-75-5
   1. Spiritual   2. New Thought   3. Self Help
   II. Title

Library of Congress Control Number: 2012930470
       Printed in the United States of America

10 9 8 7 6 5 4 3 2 1

Table of Contents

Introduction 1
Abundance 3
Acceptance 4
Adam and Eve 5
Affirmations 5
Akashic Records 7
A-Musing 7
Angels 8
Anti-Christ 9
Ascension 9
Astral Plane 10
Astrology 10
At-One-Ment 10
Attachments 11
Attraction 12
Avatars 13
Awareness 13
Baptism 14
Beatitudes 15
Belief 19
Bible 21
Blessings 23
Bliss 24
Blood 24
Body 25
Born Again 25
Brotherhood 26
Burning Bush 26
Cause and Effect 27
Cellular Theology 27
Chemicalization 28
Choices 29
Christ 30
Christ Consciousness 31
Christianity 32
Christmas 33
Christ Principle 34
Coma Consciousness 34
Comparative Religions 35
Consciousness 35
Cosmic Christ 36
Cosmic 2x4 36
Cosmic Net 37

Cosmology	38
Cross	38
Death/Transition	40
Denials	40
Denominations	41
Dis-ease	41
Divine Guidance	42
Divine Ideas	42
Divine Order	43
Divine Substance	45
Dogma	45
Dominion	46
Doubting Thomas Effect	47
Drive-By Theology	47
Each-Consecutive-Moment-Of-Now	49
Easter	49
Ego	51
Embedded Theology	51
Enlightenment	52
Entrainment	52
Error Thinking	53
Eternal Life	55
Evil	55
Evolution	56
Experience	56
Faith	57
The Fall	59
False Prophets	59
Fasting	60
Fate	60
Fear	61
First Coming	62
Forgiveness	62
Four Horsemen of the Apocalypse	64
Garden of Eden	65
Genesis	65
Giving	65
God	66
God's Will	67
Good Samaritan	68
Gospels	69
Grace	69
Gratitude	69
Guardian Angels	71
Happiness	72
Harmony	73
Healing	73

Heaven	75
Hell	76
Holy City	77
Holy Spirit	77
Hope	78
Humankind	78
Identity	79
Illusion of Separation	81
Immortality	81
Immaculate Conception	81
Incarnation	82
Inconvenient Truth	82
Indwelling Spirit	83
Inner Peace	83
Intelligent Design	84
Intention Deficit Disorder	84
Interfaith Traditions	85
Irreconcilable Differences	86
Jalopied Spirituality	87
Jerusalem Effect	87
Jesus	87
John 3:16	89
John 8:12	89
John 14:14	89
Joy	90
Judgment Day	91
Karma	92
Kindness	92
Kingdom of Heaven	92
Kingdom of God	93
Kundalini	93
Lack Consciousness	94
Law of Mind Action	95
Light	95
Literal Interpretations	96
Lord's Supper	97
Love	97
Luke 18:18; 20-24	99
Materialism	100
Matthew 13:12	101
Meditation	101
Metaphysical Malpractice	102
Metaphysics	103
Mental Kudzu	103
Mind Action	104
Miracles	105
Money	106

Mt. Sinai	107
Mysticism	107
Namaste	109
Negative Thinking	109
Neuro-Theology	110
Omnipresence, Omnipotence, Omniscience. Omni-activity	111
Oneness	111
Only Begotten Son	113
Optical Delusions	113
Original Sin	114
Pain	115
Palm Sunday	115
Peace	116
Peace Be Still	117
Pediatric Theology	117
Pentecost	117
Perceived Obstacles	118
Personality	119
Philosopher's Stone	119
Practicing the Presence	120
Prayer	122
Present Moments	124
Prosperity	124
Proverbs 6:6	127
Proverbs 23:7	128
Questions	129
Rainbow	130
Red Sea	130
Reincarnation	131
Religion	132
Religious Victrolas	134
Rest	134
Resurrection	135
Revelation 14:22	136
Revelation 21:21b	136
Righteousness	136
Ritual	137
Romans 8:28	137
Sabbath	138
Sacrifice	139
Salvation	139
Satan	140
Science	140
Second Coming	141
Self	142
Self-Knowledge	143
Sense Consciousness	143

Sermon on the Mount	144
Serpent	144
Service	144
Sin	145
Skin School	146
Son of Man	146
Song of Solomon (Song of Songs) 2:15	147
Speaking in Tongues	147
Spirit	147
Spiritual Apps	148
Spiritual Cataracts	149
Spiritual Echo-nomics	150
Spiritual Economics	150
Spiritual Growth	151
Spiritual Hydration	154
Spirituality	154
Spiritual Obstetrics	154
Spiritual Orthopedics	155
Spiritual Practice	155
Spiritual Purpose	157
Spiritual Teachers	158
Still Small Voice	158
Struggle	159
Suffering	159
Superman Christ	160
Thanksliving	161
Third Coming	161
Thought Power	161
Tithing	163
Transcendence	164
Transformation	164
Tree of Knowledge of Good and Evil	164
Tree of Life	165
Trinity	165
Truth	166
Truth Principles	167
Unforgivable Sin	168
Unity	168
Universality	170
Universal Substance	170
Universe	171
Unquiet City	172
Violence	173
Virgin Birth	173
Vow	173
"Wait" Lifting	174
Walking the Talk	174

Walking on Water 174
War.. 175
Wealth 176
White Light.. 176
Wholeness.. 177
Widowhood.. 177
Winged Globe 177
Wisdom.. 178
Word of God 179
Work 179
World 180
World of Appearances.. 180
World Peace 181
Worship... 181
Worthiness 181
X-Factor.. 182
Yoke 183
Zeal 183

*May you live at the speed of your Christ Consciousness,
as you walk the Spiritual path
on practical feet!*

Introduction

You will discover in these pages that we adamantly and enthusiastically invite you to realize that spiritual enlightenment must not be thought of as an attainment that is accomplished only by a handful of extraordinarily gifted and favored adepts who have exceptional mystical abilities.

We believe that tens of millions of people have been misled by the dogmatic assertion that Jesus is the only one who is divine. What has been over-looked entirely is the recorded statements by the Christ as Jesus himself that showed he focused on our (humankind's) innate divinity. We believe that the same Christ Presence that expressed Itself in human form as Jesus of Nazareth 2,000 years ago is the same Christ Presence that expresses Itself as us (humankind) today!

This "straight talk" book is a reflection on how much we unapologetically believe in humankind's innate divinity. In A to Z fashion we have collected 'sound bytes' from the Sunday morning messages we have delivered during our first seven years in the pulpit ministry.

As you will see, most of our views fall well outside of the pediatric theology espoused by mainstream faith traditions. Our views will no doubt push both spiritual and religious hot buttons. Some are intended to be downright edgy and thought provoking to rattle the comforted and comfort the rattled. Quite a few show our orientation to be more spiritual than religious, and just as many show how 'unplugged' Bil and Cher can be. However, all of our perspectives are intended to help readers connect with the innermost level of their being which is their Christ Self, their Authentic Self, their SuperSelf ™.

As you read each of our 'straight talk' views, allow yourself to be open-minded to the implications of transcendental theology, unshackled by tossing off the blinders created by the embedded theology you grew up with, and enthusiastic about the insights gained from the neurotheology and science overtones which underwrite many of our out-of-the-box opinions.

We know that you, like us, are on a spiritual journey. We are all doing our best to connect the proverbial dots, intending to make sense out of our human experience. Plato used the expression *heautou epimeleisthai* (care of oneself) when he encouraged us to think seriously about soul growth. For us, the care of oneself requires — no, demands — conscientious, disciplined effort to align our human self with our Christ Self. Simply put it means becoming the best Christ we can be.

So, we prefer mountaintops to valleys, green lights to red lights, sunny days to cloudy ones, open-mindedness to close mindedness, spirituality to religion, Truth instead of error, growth instead of stagnation. We have found that spiritual growth is not stunted by unanswered questions but by unquestioned answers. That being said, we have found it necessary to question traditional religious views that perpetuate the myth of an anthropomorphic God in the sky who favors some and punishes others. We also don't subscribe to religious teachings that cause people to cling to destructive dogma or teachings that sell fear and guilt as their chief commodities. And we certainly aren't fans of the exclusivity, prejudice, and arrogance which seem to define orthodox faith traditions.

Finally, we believe people trust straight talk and know what straight talk is. They may not always find it pleasant, but they respect it and value the 'authentegrity' of straight talk. We hope you'll feel the same way about the 'authentegrity' of our straight talk. We have your best interests — and humankind's best interests — in mind. It's time for transparency in politics, religion, medicine, the world of business, and all aspects of human affairs. We believe humankind is ready for Truth, honesty, unity, and cooperation. As Unity ministers, we feel obligated to do the same with our line of work. This book represents our intention to straighten out the curves and fill in the gaps of our chosen profession.

Abundance

We feel abundance in direct proportion to that which we can emotionally do without. We need no thing to complete us. It is the attachment to things which depletes us. (B)

We are pre-wired for abundance. Abundance is part of our spiritual DNA. Have faith in your Divine connection. Have faith that your good is only one thought, one affirmation, one action away. (C)

> *Virtually all the blocks to our abundant flow are rooted in subconscious issues. By definition, we are unaware of things in our subconscious. The only way we become aware of them is when they manifest through our thoughts, words, and actions. So it makes sense to begin to pay serious attention to our thoughts, words, and actions, so we can identify the useless baggage we are carrying around in our subconscious, and get rid of it! (C)*

As a matter of spiritual fact, your greater good is never more than a thought away! It's closer than the objects that appear in your rearview mirror. It's as close as your next breath. It's as close as your next thought, intention, word, choice, or action. It's as close as the book you are holding. (B)

If you are having less than perfect experiences in your finances, your relationships, your work, your health, your attitude, your life ~ just know that it is simply an outer manifestation of what is going on in your subconscious ... and you have the power to get in there and make a change! (C)

Acceptance

There is a close relationship between acceptance and tolerance. The difference requires discernment and understanding. Since we are spiritual beings in human form it may appear we should accept what outer appearances 'toss' at us. The Truth of us is that we are whole and perfect at the level of Spirit. So why should we accept dis-ease, illness, hardship, war, prejudice, or any other limiting human condition. I would encourage us to learn to tolerate, and not own (accept), those things which are not the Truth of us in our striving to become aware that we are indivisibilized expressions of the Christ at the point of us. (B)

The more you accept the dance *of* life the better you can dance *with* life. Sometimes you can waltz through challenges, other times you find yourself in a tango with the surprises life throws at you. Sometimes you can swing from one experience to another; other times you simply quick step your way out of interesting situations. (C)

Adam and Eve

We must move from our 'Adam and Eve consciousness' and work toward our 'Jesus and Magdalene consciousness' to position ourselves for Christhood. (B)

The deep theological question that holds the answers to the universe: Did Adam and Eve have belly buttons? (C)

Affirmations

Remember, things don't become true because we affirm them; we affirm them because they are Truth! So be sure your affirmations are always grounded in Truth Principles. (C)

Whenever you say affirmations, visualize positive outcomes, meditate and lift up prayers, you are stepping out of powerlessness and vulnerability. You are becoming more *"response-able."* (C)

If we use Mother Nature's echoes as a metaphor, hearing the same repetition of words over and over again turns out to be a powerful transformational tool. Repeating the same words over and over again, as in positive affirmations and mantras, is what I call 'spiritual echo-nomics.' (B)

Instead of affirming a specific outcome, try affirming the essence of what you want. For example, instead of affirming that you get a raise, affirm that you are financially free, with all your bills paid and plenty to share and spare. Instead of saying, "I no longer suffer from asthma," affirm "I have now transcended all patterns of illness. I am happy, healthy, and whole!" (C)

The brain does not simply gather and stockpile information as a computer's hard drive does. When we hear the same words, and repeat the same words, and think the same thoughts often enough, they become grooved in our consciousness and rewire our brain's neurostructures. (B)

Affirmations and denials are spiritual tweets. Imagine if Jesus would have had a Twitter account back then. One of his disciples could have tweeted Jesus' messages and sermons. Jesus could have had hundreds of thousands of people follow him on Twitter. (C)

Never say anything, no matter how true it may look on the surface, that you do not want to see manifest in your life. Think about this for a minute. It forces you to be really aware of what you are saying. Even something as simple as "I am so tired" or "I'm broke." You don't want to see those things manifest, so don't say them! And by becoming aware of what you are saying, you are also becoming aware of what you are thinking! (C)

Affirmations launch a powerful vocal vibration that holds the key to unbelievable spiritual growth that leads to your ability to divinely order your experience. (C)

No matter how deeply embedded we may feel in lack consciousness, no matter how much we are perceiving separation, no matter how depressed or sick or angry we feel, we are only a "Can you hear me now?" away. The moment we acknowledge our oneness, we are connected! There is no such thing as a dropped call! (C)

Akashic Records

Because the Akashic Records are an 'aetheric library' imprinted on an omnipresent *akasha* (a soniferous ether), we can mentally 'Google' all of the past, present, and future knowledge of the universe anytime we want when we are in certain states of heightened consciousness. Depending on our psychic sensitivity and Akashic interests, we can even 'bookmark' various knowledge banks so the information is available to us instantly. (B)

The Akashic Records, like the modern day Internet, are the equivalent of the ancient Library of Alexandria. (B)

A-Musing

I believe it inappropriate to even think about creativity, let alone attempt to measure it, without considering the set of conditions which seem to be responsible for 'teasing out' the Muse. This constelled set of conditions usually produces a breakthrough moment — one which has all of the necessary and sufficient conditions to magnetize creative ideas from their Source, the Kingdom of Heaven. (B)

Life experiences are our pallets because we can use them to color our future. (B)

I love to color outside the lines because there's a lot more room to grow there. I guess that's why I'm attracted to metaphysics. (B)

We must never allow dogma to tamp down our exploration into higher thought. (C)

Angels

Angels are highly evolved spiritual ideas and insights. They are to be welcomed and nurtured. (C)

Angels are Spirit's mRNA. (B)

Angels are at work in amazing ways in our lives. Sometimes they do their work as invisible beings; other times they are disguised as people we know; sometimes they appear as challenging individuals from whom we can learn and grow as Spiritual beings. Always assume you are with an angel and act accordingly! (C)

Anti-Christ

The Anti-Christ is our error-filled thoughts elevated to a discordant belief system that refuses to acknowledge our oneness with the Christ of us. An anti-Christ mentality sees separation, breeds separation, and leads to a life of unnecessary isolation from Spirit. (B)

Anti-Christs are the ideas that come from the shadow side of our human nature. (C)

Most people equate beings like Adolf Hitler, Joseph Stalin, Osama bin Laden, Saddam Hussein, etc. as incarnations of the Anti-Christ. The truth is that each one of us demonstrates Anti-Christ behavior whenever we purposefully, by thought or action, oppose Christ's teachings. (B)

Ascension

Every time a worldly thought or inclination rises to its spiritual octave we experience an ascension in consciousness. When our consciousness is filled with Christed thoughts, the degree of our ascension will be based on the quality of those thoughts. At some point in our spiritual unfoldment we will not need a physical form as we ascend from one cusp of awareness to another. (B)

Astral Plane

The levels of consciousness, dimensions of being, and spiritual planes are endless. Each is underwritten by a different vibration of the Infinite Intelligence we call God. We have access to these vibrations as spiritual beings in whatever dimension of being we find ourselves. The astral plane is one such dimension. It is less dense than the physical plane we inhabit as human beings. The boundaries between the interpermeating dimensions are simply a matter of consciousness. (B)

Astrology

The starry vault of the night skies is an open book to twin cosmologies: the physical universe's and ours. (C)

We are astrological melting pots of individual consciousnesses becoming aware of ourselves. And our present condition (concept of ourselves) is astronomically configured with each choice we make. The 'signs' we create can become milestones or millstones in each incarnation we manufacture. (B)

At-One-Ment

Our true work is to become 'at one' with the Christ of us. This 'at-one-ment' is expressed through our prayers, meditations, affirmations, denials (refusals to give power to outer appearances), and unselfish service to humankind. (C)

We enter into the grace of atonement every time we 'entrain' ourselves toward the vibrational power of the Christ indivisibilized as us. Each spiritual thought, every Christ-centered intention, each step into our superconscious awareness moves us into at-one-ment with our divine nature. (B)

Attachments

Humankind's attachment to material wealth, status, money, power, and prestige has enslaved millions of people to the lure of outer appearances. Our tendency toward gold fever has left us with lead feet when it comes to choosing spirituality over materiality. (B)

Only when we release our attachment to the outcome can we truly experience the amazing benefits of Truth Principles at work in our lives. (C)

Attraction

The New Thought mantra "thoughts held in mind produce after their kind" has been misunderstood and used as a manipulative toy by prosperity 'salespeople' who only have hip pocket interest in the outcome. The Truth is thoughts held in mind produce SIMILAR THOUGHTS after their kind. (C)

Avatars

Divine ideas are mentalistic 'avatars' which appear to us when we raise our consciousness to the 'Kingdom within us.' They flow out of Divine Order as spiritual guideposts to help us manifest good on the physical plane. These 'incarnated mentations' can inaugurate both personal and global prosperity. Those in tune with their Christ natures have access to these 'avatars' each-consecutive-moment-of-now. (B)

Awareness

We must not consider the limits of our current awareness as the parameters of all there is to perceive. We are multi-dimensional, multi-storied beings of Light. Our awareness is blurred by the beliefs and assumptions we've bought into. Limits in perception will cease to exist when we unlock our perceptual filters. (B)

We must awaken to the Truth that we are God expressing as the Christ at the point of us. It is this awakening that will create peace on earth. (C)

Baptism

When we cleanse our consciousness of error thoughts and inclinations we are baptized. Every time we pull ourselves out of the illusion of our separation from Spirit we experience a baptism. Each time we raise a worldly thought to its spiritual essence we are baptized. When we lift ourselves out of the negativity of the moment we are baptized. Baptism is not so much of an event as it is a process of spiritual unfoldment. (B)

Instead of arguing about which method of baptism is the best — i.e., immersion, sprinkling, christening — we need to focus on the essence of what baptism represents: the cleansing of error consciousness. Until we recognize that, it does not matter what ritual we practice. It will remain only a ritual. (C)

Beatitudes

#1: The 1st Beatitude in its literal interpretation says: *"Blessed are the poor in spirit: for theirs is the kingdom of heaven."* The root word that is translated "spirit" comes from the word *ruach* which is more accurately translated "pride, or narcissistic pride." The second half of the 1st Beatitude says: *"for their's is the Kingdom of Heaven."* Now keep in mind that 'heaven' is not a place we go to but a state we grow to! Heaven is our super-consciousnessness — which we are only beginning to understand. The root word for heaven, which is the Aramaic word Jesus would have used, means "expanding spiritual potential." This is what we believe Jesus is saying in this 1st Beatitude: *"We are enriched when we lack narcissistic pride, when we are teachable, when we are open and receptive to eternal truths, when we practice humility — and it is from that level of consciousness that we shall expand our understanding so we can fulfill our divine potential."* (B)

#2: The 2nd Beatitude, in its literal translation says: *"Blessed are they that mourn; for they shall be comforted."* This has usually been interpreted to mean that sorrow and sadness are virtues and that we will be comforted when we get to heaven. Sorrow and sadness are not virtues. They are mournful states of being. We are not put here to be sorrowful. The Christ as Jesus said he (the Christ within) came (incarnated) that we might have life and have it more abundantly. When we take a closer look at the 2nd Beatitude it reveals this Truth: *"Blessed, enriched, are those who yearn for a closer relationship with their Christ Self for they are guaranteed unlimited opportunities for soul growth."* (C)

#3: The 3rd Beatitude, as it is generally written says: *"Blessed are the meek; for they shall inherit the earth."* As it is normally understood, meek means modest, resigned, submissive, self-abasing. It suggests a willingness to 'be seen and not heard.' To willingly submit to authority.

To be compliant and silent. It promises us that we will be blessed if we are submissive and self-abased! It implies that submissive, withdrawn people will inherit the earth. We think not! We're fair students of history and current events and I can tell you meek, submissive, withdrawn people, no matter how nice they are, seem to be followers and not leaders. They don't run for President. They aren't world leaders or CEO's of mega-corporations. They don't coach sports teams or stand out in a crowd. They aren't top-selling salespeople. The word meek is a mistranslation. It is a categorical boo boo! The more accurate translation of the word *praeis* has an undeniable connotation of 'nonresistance' or 'unrestrained receptivity.' And earth, as it is used in this Beatitude means our 'waking consciousness.' So 'inherit the earth' has nothing to do with world conquest and the wars and politics that go with it! We believe this Beatitude means: *"Blessed are those who are nonresistant, who are unrestrained in their receptivity to their divinity; for they shall inherit a waking consciousness grounded in Truth principles."* (B)

#4: The 4th Beatitude, as it is generally written says: *"Blessed are they that hunger and thirst after righteousness; for they shall be filled."* Righteousness, metaphysically interpreted, means 'right thinking.' It means spiritually-attuned thinking. It implies keeping our thoughts at a spiritual octave instead of at a religious pitch. So we believe the 4th Beatitude says: *"Blessed are those who dedicate themselves to "Christed thinking, being, and doing for they shall unfold their divine potential."* (C)

#5: The 5th Beatitude, as it is usually stated, reads: *"Blessed are the merciful; for they shall obtain mercy."* To have mercy is a wonderful human trait. Mercy, in all of its forms — kindness, tenderness, empathy, leniency, and clemency — is a soulful thing to offer anyone. However, the word mistranslated as 'merciful' from the original Aramaic is *rakhma* which means 'unconditional love.' It means loving people the way they are regardless of who they are, how they are, where they are, and why they are. We believe the 5th Beatitude, correctly interpreted says: *"Blessed are those who offer unconditional love; for they shall receive unconditional love."* (B)

#6: In its traditional interpretation, the 6th Beatitude is a heart-centered message. As it is commonly understood it reads: *"Blessed are the pure in heart; for they shall see God."* This translation implies that if we are good, decent, moral, and virtuous human beings, we will see God when we stand before the Pearly Gates. Devoting ourselves to 'pure living' is certainly a good thing to do. However, the implication that we will stand in the presence of an anthropomorphic God in the sky one day misses the central teaching of this Beatitude. In the original Aramaic, the correct translation for *dadcean* is not "pure in heart" per se. It's more correctly translated as 'spiritual perspective.' It's referring to an enlightened mind. A mind centered in super-conscious awareness. A mind that values the spiritual over the material. The word 'see' as it is used in the standard interpretation of the 6th Beatitude is a mistranslation of the word *mikhazoun* which means 'comprehend.' So, the 'seeing' implied here is not physical sight, but an internal 'seeing.' We believe a more correct interpretation of the 6th Beatitude is: *"Blessed are those who see things from a Christ perspective; for they shall comprehend their innate divinity."* (C)

#7: A literal interpretation of the 7th Beatitude says: *"Blessed are the peacemakers, for they shall be called the children of God."* 'Peacemakers' is a mistranslation of the Aramaic expression *abdey shlama* which means "through service, work conscientiously to find inner peace." Metaphysically, children represent divine ideas, and childhood symbolizes our Christ potential. So being true to the original Aramaic meaning and adding a pinch of metaphysics, we believe the 7th Beatitude says: *"Blessed are those who conscientiously follow a spiritual practice for they shall experience inner peace and actualize their Christ potential."* (C)

#8: The 8th Beatitude as it is traditionally translated says: *"Blessed are they that have been persecuted for righteousness' sake; for theirs is the kingdom of heaven."* Unfortunately, this mistranslation has led hundreds of millions of people through the ages to accept martyrdom and to wear victimization and poverty as badges of honor. Essentially it has been interpreted to mean that we are blessed when we are persecuted for being Christian. The key word that is mistranslated as 'persecuted' actually comes from the Aramaic word *dea-tredepo* which means 'to restrain from temptation.' The only persecution this Beatitude is talking about takes place between our ears. And our persecutors are errant thoughts, stale belief systems, and self-defeating habits which are the chief characteristics of a selfish, materialistic, egocentric consciousness. The word righteousness means 'right thinking.' The 'kingdom of heaven' is a metaphysical idiom that stands for 'our innate divinity.' It is this innate divinity that is the altar of our spiritually-attuned consciousness. It's a spiritual Petri dish that grows divine ideas. The 8th Beatitude, reinterpreted and brushed off says: *"Blessed are those who do not allow worldly temptations to deter them from right thinking; for they shall honor their innate divinity."* (B)

#9: The traditional 9th Beatitude, in its mistranslated version says: *"Blessed are you when people insult you, persecute you and falsely say all kinds of evil against you because of me. Rejoice and be glad, because great is your reward in heaven, for in the same way they persecuted the prophets who were before you."* This mistranslation asks us to wear reproach and persecution like badges of honor and promises us our suffering will be rewarded when we step through the Pearly Gates. And the justification for taking this abuse is that our loved ones, and friends, and Biblical prophets all went through the same gauntlet of misery for their faithfulness. So, be tough like they were, it instructs us! The truth is the reproaches, persecutions, and false accusations mentioned in this Beatitude are all mental hiccups that take place in our heads. Cher and I believe the 9th Beatitude says: *"Blessed are those who press on, who do not allow the inertia of past programming and embedded theology to dampen their spirituality. Their devotion to right thinking will pay off."* (B)

So, there you have the Beatitudes presented to you with an attitude, an attitude which comes from the belief that the Truth will make you free: free from an embedded theology based on mistranslations, and free from the misdirection caused by those mistranslations.

We've added another Beatitude, a 10th Beatitude, to sum up our position on the need to move beyond the limitations of literal interpretations of sacred scripture.

Bonus #10: The 10th Beatitude says: *"Blessed are those who have the moxie to forget conventional misconceptions they learned about the Bible and God; for they shall become enlightened."*

Belief

Spiritual beliefs are like a mental shampoo, they wash the materialistic film off our thinking. (C)

Strongly asserted spiritual beliefs blow the circuits of pragmatic, closed minds. These 'out of the realm of logic' beliefs will always confound those who base their thinking on stagnant, walled beliefs (convention) instead of spiritual insights. (B)

In order to grow spiritually we must leave formaldehyde beliefs and atrophied dogmas behind. We must be ready for a thought triage, a new calculus of belief. We must also understand that spiritual growth needs landing gears as well as wings. (B)

If we say we believe everyone is divine within, we need to be sure we treat every person that way. If we believe we are connected to Divine Substance, we need to live in alignment with that belief. If we recognize the power of meditation and prayer, we need to be sure we are making time to spend there! (C)

The Christ as Jesus said in John 14:13: *"Whatever you declare in my name ... whatever you declare in my name ...*(our emphasis) *... I will do it!"* We believe that means whatever we declare, whatever we affirm, whatever we claim, whatever we envision, whatever we believe from our Christ Consciousness shall become our experience. The historical Christ as Jesus said it 2,000 years ago and the Christ as us wants us to declare that same Truth confidently and faithfully and joyfully today! (B)

Beliefs are ego filters that color our experience. We manufacture them to make sense out of our human dramas. Sometimes we hide behind them. Sometimes we change them when we find the courage to look beyond the obvious. Our spiritual growth depends on our being able to look beyond the obvious. (C)

Prayer, faith, positive affirmations, visualization, healing touch, meditation, and denying the power of outer appearances are all powerful Placebos. They work because they are the out-picturing of our consciousness; they are the products of Mind Action; they are mind over molecules! (B)

We can SAY we believe we live in an abundant universe, that we always have everything we need at the point of need, that there is plenty to share and plenty to spare ... but if our choices don't support and feed those beliefs, we will not see them manifest in our life! In order to experience the highest, most elevated manifestation of our spiritual laws of prosperity and abundance, we need to make conscious choices, with serious intention. (C)

Bible

The Bible is the most complete, unadulterated, uncensored, absolutely telling, uncannily relevant, and highly revealing story of our evolving spiritual consciousness. (B)

There are many translations and interpretations of the Bible — which is to be expected. After all, it chronicles our spiritual unfoldment. As we grow, our understanding of sacred scripture grows. (C)

There is only one story in the Bible: It is the story of our evolving spiritual consciousness. And that story is about our using more won't power than will power when it comes to "practicing the Presence." (B)

Those who fixate on merely a literal interpretation of sacred scripture generally find it difficult to connect all of the theological dots. That could explain why they end up with a linear, dogmatically superficial religious perspective. A more metaphorical, esoteric, or metaphysical perspective would help them take off the parochial blinders and deepen their theology. (B)

Any true Bible scholar has to admit that hundreds of legitimate manuscripts were deleted by a panel of Constantine groupies in 325 C.E. The council tossed divinely inspired texts that would have benefitted humankind immensely, texts like the Book of Thomas, The Gospel of Mary, the Book of Levi, the original Apostle's Creed, the Book of Enoch. Current Christian Bibles will continue to be incomplete until and unless other divinely inspired and deserving sacred writings are included. (C)

Cher and I are seldom satisfied with literal translations of scripture because many of them are literally mistranslations. While a literal text's face value may justify its religious worth, its spiritual value is lost. (B)

You know who the Great Villain is in the New Testament don't you? It's not Herod, and it's not Pontius Pilate. And it certainly isn't Judas. The Roman soldier who flogged Jesus and the Romans who made him carry the cross aren't the Great Villains either. Neither is the Roman who drove the spikes into his hands and feet or the Roman who gave Jesus vinegar when Jesus cried, "I thirst." The Roman who thrust a spear in Jesus' side isn't 'the Villain' either. The notorious Villain in the New Testament, and in all sacred writings for that matter, is none other than the selfish shadow side of the human personality. It's the side that worships physical form and loves material things. (B)

Blessings

Send light, love, peace, joy, hope, and all kinds of virtual blessings to others, no matter who they are, where they are, or what they are experiencing. Lift others up on a regular basis. (C)

Whenever you feel absolutely frustrated, blocked, or stuck, that is the very time for you to focus on your blessings. As you allow your thoughts to give complete attention to the abundant good in your life, you will attract from within the Divine Ideas that can propel you to solutions. (C)

If you have ever said things like or agree with someone else saying things like "the cancer blessed me," or "lime disease blessed me," or "a broken nose blessed me," or "this heart attack was the best thing that ever happened to me," or "getting fired blessed me," you are giving your power away and assigning a blessing on something that doesn't deserve to be blessed! What blessed you was not what happened to you but how you responded to what happened to you. (B)

What we bless multiplies and grows. A blessing means to confer prosperity upon. So, we must always bless, confer prosperity upon, what we want to manifest. We have the incredible power to confer prosperity upon everything, everyone, and every circumstance that comes to us — and in so doing, we create an unending ripple effect of prosperity and abundance. (C)

Bliss

Happiness, harmony and inner knowing are not condiments; they're the main course, the chief ingredients in bliss. (C)

Unfortunately, the unenlightened miss 'bliss' because they consider it too airy fairy to be a real emotion. Nevertheless, one can get lost in cosmic bliss and touch a dimension of being that reminds us we are more than flesh and blood human beings with a limited appreciation for realness. (B)

Amusement is regional, bliss extends over our entire beingness. (C)

Blood

It is the revitalized, purified blood which is produced by our higher conscious connection with Spirit that elevates our vibration above dis-ease and any other human limitation. Once an individual's blood is enriched in this way, the blood of the entire human race is lifted up. Each time a human being elevates his or her consciousness the human 'superconscious bloodline' is enriched beyond measure. (B)

Just as blood courses through our veins, Truth courses through our consciousness. Jesus raised the level of purity in his blood by becoming consciously one with his Christ Nature. His neurology was also cleansed and quickened when his human self aligned completely with his Christ Self. The potency of his spilled blood is a gift to all of us. It opens the door to our collective blood transfusion. (C)

Body

Our human body is a garment we wear to clothe our choice to become physical beings. (C)

Our physical body is our biological address. It is the 'somatic spacesuit' we have constructed to house our particular version of Spirit. (B)

Born Again

The phrase "born again" is referring, in a very real sense, to a kind of spiritual obstetrics. (B)

The phrase 'born again,' metaphysically speaking, means 'to transcend sense attachments' or 'move beyond material appetites.' It means to elevate our awareness to a higher level of awareness. It means to realize there is no separation between us and Spirit. (B)

Brotherhood

It is Cher's and my belief that if people would truly accept the Truth that they are divine beings in human form, and that they are God expressing Godness as them, we could erase hunger, and disease, and war, and crime, and violence off the face of the earth. There would truly be peace on earth and goodwill — God's will — to all people whether they are white or black, Asian or African, tall or short, gay or strait, differently-abled or able-bodied, rich or poor, Duke fans or Carolina fans, chocolate lovers or pizza addicts. (B)

We all come from the same Source. We are all embodiments of the same Spirit. It's time we took better care of one another. (C)

Burning Bush

Metaphysically, Moses' burning bush experience stands for an extremely powerful transformation in consciousness. It is the fiery rise of the serpentine energies within us that burn off the dross of error. We will experience our own 'burning bush' when our consciousness is purified of all error thoughts and inclinations. We will have reached a high state of enlightenment. But like Moses, we still have a lot of work to do. Even mystics pay taxes and occasionally need to de-friend someone off their Facebook account. From a 'burning bush' state of awareness we can free our thoughts (Israelites) from the darkness of duality and separation (Egypt). (B)

Cause and Effect

We re-cause our human experience every time we make a choice. If we don't like what we're manifesting — the effects — we can make another choice, that is, re-cause our experience. (C)

Quantum physicists know that effects can precede their causes. That finding is the universe telling us that our concept of cause and effect is relative to our degree of enlightenment. (B)

Cellular Theology

Each cell, every molecule, each atom is a sacred tabernacle of Spirit. These sacred tabernacles are connected. There is no denominational sparing. Their biology is their theology. When we realize the significance of this invisible connection we will honor the human soul's relationship to Spirit. When we acknowledge this connection, from soul to cell, our body becomes the highly-charged sacred ground of our being. When we achieve this perfect synchrony we experience the inner peace, joy, health, and wholeness which are the Truth of us. (B)

Chemicalization

Chemicalization is a sort of spiritual floss. It loosens the crust of old tapes, conventional assumptions, and subconscious thought patterns and helps us clean up our act. As we become more aware of the dissonance between the spiritual us and the material us we experience a depth charge of inner transformative energies that intensify and lead to what can be a rather volatile process of interior cleansing and purification. The fusion of enlightened thought and stale belief systems causes an internal combustion that sends specks and flecks of our ego's insecurities to the surface. This tumultuous inner growth process is called chemicalization and the interior transformation that occurs penetrates all levels of our being, purging us from error. (B)

When you receive a new piece of life-changing information that blows your mind, your old programming resists the new information and you may experience an internal upheaval. Chemicalization shows up in lots of different ways, and if you don't know about it, you might think you are going backwards because you are experiencing unexplained nervousness, uncharacteristic impatience, headaches, the return of old habits that you thought you had overcome, weeping for no apparent reason, etc. No worries! You are purging the old, making room for your new level of awareness! (C)

Chemicalization is 'spiritual Alka Seltzer.' It settles the rough and tumble growth curve that new spiritual insights force on our old life patterns. (B)

Quantum turbulence is the name physicists give to the chaotic motion (flow) of eddies and vortices (called whirlpools) in gases or liquids. Under normal conditions all fluids have a resistance to flow (viscosity). This turbulence, this burning off the dross of error, from a spiritual point of view, is called chemicalization. It is a necessary turbulence because our consciousness is ground zero for our spiritual growth. Chemicalization is caused by new spiritual insights that create cognitive dissonance which upsets old patterns of thinking, being, and doing. It sends us into inner turmoil (turbulence), a time of questioning, soul searching, and finally into an enlightened perspective. (B)

Choices

Choice is a magic wand to the mind. (C)

Choices work like echoes, they return the volume of the choice; the noisier the choice, the noisier the feedback. (B)

You will manage your life when you manage yourself, and you will manage yourself when you manage your choices. (C)

Eeny, Meeny, Miny, MORE! We all make thousands of choices every day, and all too often we make those choices by default rather than by intention. Just hang out at a coffee shop, and you will realize that lots of people spend more energy and time choosing how they want their coffee fix than they do choosing how they want to experience their life! But it is time to turn that around! Over the years, we have learned one critically important lesson: It doesn't really matter what your values are. It doesn't even matter what your beliefs are—or your goals. What is truly important—what makes the difference—is each and every choice you make! (C)

We are kept in sync by the acupuncture of our wise choices. (B)

We can choose to go within or do without. (C)

We excel toward our Christhood or decelerate one choice at a time. Our enlightenment comes from hunkered-down Christed choices. (B)

Our choices do not hang out in the past or wait for us in the future. All choices are present tense moments. (C)

Christ

Christ is Godness indivisiblized as us. However we must recognize It, unfold It, and become consciously one with It to fulfill the human phase of our enlightenment. (B)

The Christ in us is our hope of glory; the Christ as us is our evidence of attunement (glory). It is not enough to be Christ at the point of us. We must become awakened, energetic, active Christs. (B)

The Golden Buddha of Tibet is a perfect metaphor for the Christ within each of us. Covered with the clay of our humanity, we lose sight of the precious Divinity that is within. (C)

The same Christ that expressed Itself as Jesus is the same Christ that expresses Itself as us. (B)

Since pyramids mean 'fire in the middle' we could say, without stretching it too far, that the mysterious power associated with pyramids is an apt metaphor for the mysterious, preservative, healing power of the 'fire in the middle' of us — our Christ Nature! It is the Divine Fire in our solar plexus. The Cosmic Flicker at our core, the Lux Aeterna, the Eternal Light of our Christ Self. (B)

Our true self is the Christ embodied in, as, and through us. Our task is to embody our Christ Nature. (C)

We must stop crucifying the Christ within ourselves. Instead we need to crucify our sense-addicted ego which we have allowed to perpetuate error and duality. (B)

Christ Consciousness

When we live at the speed of our Christ Consciousness, and allow that awareness to define our lives, we create a state of receptivity which magnetizes anything we need to help us be the best Christ we can be. (C)

When God (the Universal Isness) set the 'rainbow' in the sky (endowed each of us with seven powerful spiritual centers [chakras]), it was an act of great promise. It was a token of a covenant between God and we spiritual beings who have chosen yet another physical human form. Ever since then, humankind has sought to find the "pot of gold" at the end of the 'rainbow' so that we can find the health, wealth and happiness we seek. The rainbow's promise (kundalini's promise) and its treasure will not be found in the atmospherics of material pursuits but in the harmonics of the Indwelling Christ Consciousness. (B)

There is an Eastern parable which says that if you meet the Buddha on the road to your spiritual enlightenment, you must kill him. This cryptic saying is telling us that our fixation on a particular spiritual or religious path as THE answer may hinder our spiritual growth. We must always remain open to new spiritual insights so we can grow our consciousness. Our movement toward Christ Consciousness is a cumulative process of unfoldment. (C)

> *Align your consciousness with your Christ Consciousness before you do anything else, and 'all these things shall be given unto you.' What things? What things do we get when we put God first? We get things like divine ideas, inner guidance, intuitive insights, spectacular hunches, spiritual inspiration, deeper knowledge, extraordinary wisdom, laser-like discernment, a joyful outlook, happiness, confidence, and a positive attitude — things money can't buy. (B)*

Christianity

Christianity must return to its mystical and metaphysical roots or run the risk of becoming totally irrelevant. (B)

Christianity has become entirely too literal. Christendom has been dumbed down with too much dogma and too many mistranslations. (C)

I spell Christian 'Christ-I-am.' Any other spelling just doesn't make good theological sense. (B)

Christmas

Scrooge-ology is a message of transformation and release. Once we recognize our innate Divinity, we have the power to release anything that limits or blocks our good. When the Ebenezer Scrooge of us comes out of its attachment to things (its Amorite consciousness) and releases its addiction to material and monetary appetites, we can literally be transformed by the renewing of our minds. (B)

The shepherds mentioned in the Gospel Nativity account represent the humble, trustworthy, connected-to-nature thoughts we have that watch over our good and obedient intentions (symbolized by sheep). These fearless and courageous thoughts protect us from selfish and materialistic inclinations. (B)

Metaphysically speaking, the magi stand for our enlightened human will which knows it must bow to, be receptive to, our Christ Self. They came from the east, according to the literal account. The 'east' means that 'place of higher consciousness within us' — the Kingdom of God. And 'west' means our 'sense-oriented consciousness which is tied to the world of appearances.' So, our receptive human will (the magi) which springs from that place of higher consciousness within us (the east) seeks to become more enlightened so we can master the art of living (symbolized by the west)! (B)

The Advent Wreath is a circle, which symbolizes the Omnipotence, Omniscience, and Omnipresence of God, and the never-ending love we experience when we are connected in Spirit and recognize that oneness. The greenery symbolizes growth and renewal, as we renew our commitment to Truth principles and our relationship with God. The four candles around the outside represent four attitudes we foster as we move through the Christmas season: Expectation; Peace; Joy; and Love. The white candle in the center is the Christ candle, which celebrates the birth of Jesus ~ and the birth of the Christ within each of us. (C)

Christ Principle

The Christ Principle is God indivisiblized as the Perfect Idea of Godness in physicality. It is the presence of God actualized through the Christ at the point of us. (B)

Coma Consciousness

Our ego-driven, sense-oriented consciousness is wrapped up in the illusions wrought by the world of outer appearances. We call this 'walled in outlook' coma consciousness. Its worldly addictions make it difficult, and oftentimes cumbersome, for us to grow spiritually. (B)

A consciousness that dwells on sickness, lack, fear, guilt, and greed is a state of awareness that keeps us comatose and clueless as to our divine origins. It is a consciousness that needs to be resuscitated. (C)

Coma consciousness is the worship of outer appearances. It's giving dominion to material things. It's denying our divinity or taking it for granted. It's looking for hamburger when we have steak at home — the hamburger being worldly appetites, the steak being Spirit. (B)

Comparative Religions

Cher and I are members, I suppose, of a greater spiritual community who find ourselves upsetting proverbial applecarts by honoring all faith traditions, knowing the Source of their religious beliefs is the same Universal Source that underwrites our own beliefs. (B)

Consciousness

The speed of light (metaphysically speaking, refers to the aware intellect) is many times slower than the speed of our super-consciousness. It takes light approximately 7 1/2 minutes to reach earth from the sun. It only takes a nano-second for us to realize we are 'here' and the sun is 'there.' Consciousness travels a gazillion times faster than the speed of light. (B)

We need to make the conscious awareness of our divinity a habit. The more we live in that consciousness the better our chances will be to master our human experience. (C)

Verse 24 in Matthew's Gospel and verse 48 in Luke's Gospel refer to building a house on rock. Metaphysically, 'house' means "consciousness" and 'rock' means a 'strong faith foundation built on Truth principles.' It could also mean a consciousness (house) built on the knowledge that there is no separation between us and our Christ Nature (rock). (B)

Consciousness is the ground of all being. It is the unified field quantum physicists are seeking. It is the singularity that spawns multiverses and universes. (B)

Cosmic Christ

The Cosmic Christ is the universal indivisibleness of God expressing Itself in space time. Until we can comprehend the Cosmic Christ in us as us we cannot comprehend the real us. (B)

Cosmic 2x4

Place your right palm over your right ear. We have you do this because what I'm about to say is so important for your happiness and prosperity that I don't want it to go in one ear and out the other. Are you ready? Keep your hand over your ear as you read the following statements: One of the self-denigrating assumptions Cher and I invite you to compost is the belief in a cosmic 2x4 — that there is some celestial being or something 'out there' trying to get your attention to teach you an important lesson. There is no cosmic 2x4! The 'whack of clarity' between your eyes comes from your Third Eye, the inner spiritual eye, the mystical gate or portal that represents the seer in you. The 'whack' doesn't come from 'out there.' (B)

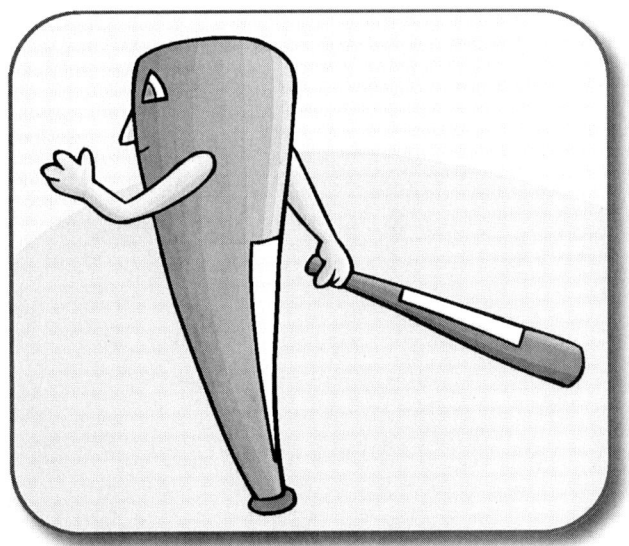

"I've been hit by a cosmic 2 x 4" is the phrase we tend to use when we run smack into an experience that feels bad, that is so sudden and shocking that it wakes us up. It could be a serious illness, or a job challenge, or something whacky with our relationships. Or maybe it's something showing up that we thought we had long since handled! Whatever it is, it feels uncomfortable — so we use the cosmic 2x4 expression to justify it, implying that some being outside of us is trying to get our attention to teach us some important lesson! And if we don't get it the first time, look out! The whack is going to get progressively worse till we finally pay attention. We've got to get over that kind of rationalization. There is no cosmic 2x4. **We** create our 2x4 moments!(C)

Cosmic Net

In Matthew 13:47-50 Jesus' disciples cast a net into the sea, and bring up a whole bunch of stuff in it. It's chock full — but not everything is "gold." So they pull the net to shore and separate the good fish from the bad fish and other junk caught up in the net. The good fish are put in a basket, and the outcast stuff is thrown away. There's a final verse here that says, "This is how it will be at the end of the age. The angels will come and separate the wicked from the righteous and throw them into the fiery furnace, where there will be weeping and gnashing of teeth." What this is saying from a metaphysical perspective is that a higher spiritual perspective is like a "cosmic net" which catches all of our thoughts, intentions, ideas. At some point, we review these and are able, with divine wisdom and understanding, to keep the ones that serve our higher good, and discard the ones that could limit our spiritual growth. The 'weeping and gnashing of teeth' reference means that sometimes it isn't easy, because we get attached to our habits, our thoughts, our embedded theology. It is difficult to release them, and we sometimes complain, or make excuses, or resist. But when we are able to let them go, we are able to move to a whole new level of awareness of our Oneness with Spirit! (C)

Cosmology

Serious students of Truth must be willing to legitimize a shared cosmology with quantum physics and the sciences. A cosmology which holds that the origin and nature of the universe is inextricably linked with the origin and nature of our relationship with the One Reality we call by many names. That shared cosmology will be criticized. It will be misunderstood. It may even be ridiculed. But the marriage between science and spirituality, between quantum physics and prayer, between the neocortex and forgiveness, between the Hayflict limit and the sky's the limit must take place. (B)

Cross

The cross we bear is physicality. It is our human experience. As spiritual beings who have chosen a human experience we have settled for limitation and duality instead of limitlessness and conscious oneness with the Eternal Presence. It is a symbol of our skin school matriculation. The cross bar represents human consciousness, what Cher and I call coma consciousness.

The vertical bar represents Spirit's descent into human consciousness. (B)

To be crucified means to cross out error from our mortal consciousness. Every time we cross out error we come closer to consciously realizing our true nature which is divine. (C)

From a dogmatic fundamentalist perspective the cross is a gruesome religious symbol which retails guilt, sin, shame, blood, suffering, and condemnation. From a metaphysical perspective, the mud, blood, and burden of the cross misses the most important point of the Easter experience! A more esoteric view of the crucifixion takes it out of a mainstream religious guilt trip and lifts the Easter story to its spiritual significance. The crucifixion represents the crossing out of error from our consciousness. (B)

The cross reminds us of the work we still have to do to erase error from our consciousness. The cross doesn't have to be a permanent fixture in our spiritual growth. (C)

The crucifixion experience takes place in your head. That's why the crucifixion takes place on Golgotha, the place of the skull. The crucifixion is an inside job. (B)

Death/Transition

Physical death is liberation from a human experience, not the end of our conscious beingness. It reminds us that our physical body is too dense to travel to our next assignment. (C)

We take what we bring and what we've given. That is to say, at our transition we take the consciousness we've developed in this existence to our next assignment and add that 'skin school' experience to our evolving soul consciousness. Our "composite self" is given its next assignment so we can continue in our soul growth. I use the word transition instead of death because the idea of death contradicts the very teachings of Jesus, the Christ. He said if we believe in Him we shall never die. I take that promise literally. I believe that means if we honor our oneness with the Christ of us, we will keep our life vibration above the level of disintegration called death. What I find very interesting is that many churches come equipped with graveyards, which seems to support the idea that death is inevitable. (B)

Denials

Fear, doubt, reticence, denial, and other negative responses to outer appearances can limit our good when we choose to hold onto anything which separates us from our good. (C)

Denialdom, from a Unity perspective, is the refusal to give power to outer appearances, whether those appearances take the form of health challenges, lack or limitation, financial challenges, natural disasters, disappointments, work issues, relationship issues, etc. This conscious erasure of the apparent invincibility of appearances keeps us centered on the Truth that we can choose wholeness instead of negation, faith instead of fear, confidence instead of confusion, victory instead of victimhood, health instead of illness. (B)

Denials are simply our way of crossing out error by refusing to give power to anything out of alignment with Truth. Bil and I aren't saying it doesn't exist. Goodness knows, if you have a fever and are coughing, your human self is definitely experiencing a health challenge. And if you have more month left than money, your human self is experiencing lack. But the effect these experiences have on us is determined by us! We can deny any power they have over us. (C)

Denominations

The world doesn't need another religious denomination. However, a sassy, in your face, forward thinking, Truth-focused spiritual denomination could be just the right perspective we need to elevate humankind's collective consciousness to a truly enlightened level of awareness. (B)

Dis-ease

Dis-ease is the misalignment between our human self and our Christ Self. It is perpetuated by an erroneous belief in duality and separation. It is fed by our refusal to surrender to our Christ Nature. (B)

Divine Guidance

Divine Guidance is in our spiritual DNA. It springs from the omnipresence of our indivisible connection to Spirit. It is an inherited spiritual quality within us. We position ourselves to receive guidance when we raise our consciousness to its elevated spiritual pitch. Divine guidance doesn't come to us; it pours out of our divinity. (B)

Divine Ideas

Invariably, I come out of the Silence with a few ideas. They may seem weird or impractical, but I write them down and give them consideration. And if I don't have ideas, I simply affirm that Divine Ideas are flowing to me, and I release all concern and worry about this issue. Believe me, the ideas start coming! (C)

We have access to Divine Ideas because we are divine beings being human. We can receive them any time we want through our connection with Spirit. They come from our super-consciousness which warehouses our 'Inner Net' of Divine Ideas. (B)

Every Divine Idea is an opportunity of abundance, a gift of healing, a seed of joy. (C)

Don't ever think a Divine Idea is too small to be of value! The more you believe in it, persistently work it, and faithfully enhance it, the growth value can be astronomical! (C)

Divine Order

I invite you to be very careful when you refer to Divine Order as something 'out there,' something external that is rigid and imposed upon us by some celestial deity. It is omnipresent scaffolding available to us. Divine Order is not some cosmic force that acts upon us. Because Divine Order is the creative process of Mind — Idea — Expression it is an intentional act of creation. We can divinely order good or we can misapply Divine Order and create error expressions. A Divine Idea can be expressed spiritually or selfishly. Spiritually expressed it is a capital "D" Divine Idea. Selfishly expressed it is 'diddlysquat order' since a Divine Idea has been misapplied. (B)

The reason all things can work together for good is because we can work all things together for good. It is us, as extensions of the power of the Christ Presence within us, who can Divinely Order all of our earthly experiences. (C)

We can turn millstones into milestones when we turn diddlysquat order into Divine Order. Divine Order is when we divinely order our experience from the consciousness of our oneness with Spirit. Diddlysquat order is a millstone perspective. It means allowing our fractured and frightened egos to tempt us into believing that we are separated from Spirit, that we are not divine beings, and that all good things must come to an end. (B)

What we need to remember most is that we are always divinely ordering our human experience. There is always an order to what we are doing! We just don't always use it at its highest, most elevated level of consciousness. Sometimes we are Divinely Ordering our lives, and other times we are manifesting what Bil and I love to call "diddlysquat order!" (C)

If you believe you're "exactly where you're supposed to be" or "should be" because some divine puppeteer 'up there' is pulling your strings, I invite you to "stop shoulding on yourself." If you are where you are supposed to be, or should be, or ought to be, or had better be it's because you are there by right of your own consciousness — not somebody else's or something else's. If it's all in divine order it's because you have ordered it. (B)

Divine Order is our at-one-ment with Spirit demonstrating itself in human terms. (C)

How often have you heard people use this phrase as a statement of resignation. "It's all in Divine Order" meaning it's out of my hands, out of my control. It's already pre-determined by the Divine Order default police who know what's best for me. Metaphysically speaking, Divine Order is not an external God-generated fiat or something a celestial deity imposes upon us. Divine Order is not an event. It is a process. It is not a noun. It is a verb. It is not a pre-determined outcome. It is a preemptive course of action on our part, as Christed beings in human form, to manifest something visible from the invisible. (B)

Success, happiness, and prosperity work the same way because they are divinely timed! Unfortunately, many people upset the timing by holding onto their fears, doubts, assumptions, greed, material attachments, unforgiveness, and illusions of a God 'out there' who dispenses favors to some and withholds good from others. (B)

Divine Substance

Why is it so easy to believe, without a doubt, that apple seeds produce apple trees, and oranges produce orange juice — but so difficult to believe that Divine Substance produces everything we ever need in terms of manifesting our supply? In truth, all we have to do is **faith it** until we make it. (C)

Dogma

Dogma is a spiritual lobotomy. (B)

One of the covenants Cher and I have built into our Truth walks is that we don't do dogma. (B)

I look forward to the day when religion is detoxed of dogma. (C)

There has been, and continues to be, such an explosion of dogmatic fiascos that any attempt to give them even an iota of credence leads inevitably to intellectual vertigo. (B)

James Powers begins his book *Lions, Hearts, Leaping Does* with the following paraphrase from the *Book of Thomas*: "Skip the exegesis, I can do without that. Read what the verse really says." If I were paraphrasing that I would say, "Skip the junk, and give me some decent theology. That is, skip the dogma. Skip superficial interpretations of scripture." People want depth. People want life-changing relevance. People want to know what scripture really says. While exegesis has its place there's a part of us that knows there's more to scripture. (B)

People all over the world are saying, 'Skip the superficial, give me some decent theology. Give me something relevant and practical. Give me something I can use to improve my life now." (C)

The spiritual view of dogma is in reverse order. Dogma spelled backwards is 'am god.' Wasn't it the Christ as Jesus who said, "Ye are gods?" (B)

> *Dogma is nothing more than jurassic theology, asphyxiating on its own lack of depth. Thankfully, it's becoming so extinct that it's on the endangered species list. (B)*

Dominion

In Genesis 1:26 God is reported as saying, (the literalists need to explain pre-human conversation) "Let us give humans dominion over the fish of the sea, the birds of the air, over the cattle and wild animals, and over every creeping thing upon the earth." In verse 28 God blesses us humans and is reported as saying, "Be fruitful and multiply, and have dominion over all that moves on the face of the earth." From a metaphysical perspective the earth represents our human consciousness; fish (ideas); birds (higher thoughts); cattle (compliant, herd consciousness); wild animals (untamed or undisciplined instincts); creeping things (our limited or destructive inclinations). Camels weren't mentioned because they hadn't gotten over the evolutionary hump yet (I'm messing with you). So, if we choose love over error we have complete dominion over our ideas, higher thoughts, compliant attitudes, undisciplined instincts, and even our destructive inclinations. We have control over the earth — which is our egocentric consciousness! (B)

Doubting Thomas Effect

Doubts are 'spiritual recoils' which can catapult us into our next growth curve. (B)

Self-doubt can lure us into Self-denial — that's denial of our capital 'S' Self, our Christ Self. We need to doubt our doubts. (C)

Our doubts can be walls or speed bumps when it comes to our spiritual awakening. (B)

Thomas needed to see the physical proof of the risen Christ. We must move beyond the Doubting Thomas Effect, and realize that the world of appearance is nothing but smoke and mirrors! The Truth transcends our physical senses, and comes from an inner knowing that no one can destroy. (C)

Drive-By Theology

'Drive-by Theology' is diverting our attention away from a breath-takingly beautiful spiritual Truth and giving in to the first worldly temptation that comes our way. We cannot be centered in our spirituality when we pine for material attachments. We cannot be the best Christ we can be by constantly feeding our egocentric whims and material addictions. Lukewarm commitment to spiritual growth usually leads to cold feet in hot circumstances. (B)

Bil and I can't promise you a rose garden. But we promise you that once you move beyond 'drive-by theology' and apply the Truth principles you know, your human experience will be more fulfilling, more peaceful, and more joyful, despite the slings and arrows that come with human incarnation. (C)

Spiritual knowledge is 'drive-by theology' if it's not used. Saying there is only One Presence and One Power in our lives and affairs is 'drive-by theology' if we don't apply that knowledge. Affirming our good a hundred times a day but doubting if those very affirmations will work is 'drive-by theology.' Not living a prayer-conditioned life is 'drive-by theology.' (B)

There are plenty of drive-by examples: news stories about drive-by shootings; drive-by analysis of a project (which means it is casual or superficial); a drive-by medical procedure (one in which you drop into a hospital or clinic, have the procedure done, and then leave); a drive-by meal (the fun term for a fast-food drive through); drive-by hackers (those pesky people who drive through a neighborhood and access your wireless access); and even drive-by tours (where you see your favorite sights — from your seat on the bus). What do these examples have to do with our spiritual growth? Too many people have Drive-By Spiritual Experiences, where they sample a variety of spiritual practices and techniques, but never go deeper. (C)

Once you decide to go deeper and really put in the time with your spiritual enrichment, you will experience the most amazing Inner expansion — and you will be on the journey of a lifetime. (C)

Each Consecutive Moment Of Now

Each consecutive moment of now is the future becoming the present at the speed of consciousness. Most people see it as a consecutive sequence of seconds or minutes of time. However, it is more like instantaneous shifts in consciousness. (B)

> *Your incredible future has nothing to do with what you have, or what people around you are doing, or who you know, or what you are going through. It has EVERYTHING to do with HOW you choose to BE in each consecutive moment of now. Let me say that one more time: It has EVERYTHING to do with HOW you choose to BE in each consecutive moment of now. (C)*

Master teacher Jesus told us to give no thought to tomorrow. He didn't mean to just fly by the seat of our pants and never do any planning! What He meant by that was to stay focused on this moment, this day, and be very aware of the choices we are making in this moment. When we are fully present in this moment, we cannot become overwhelmed; we cannot stay depressed about the past or fearful of the future because we are only giving attention and energy to what is ours to do this moment! (C)

Easter

Metaphysically, Pontius Pilate stands for the carnal will, which also means muddy water. So, the Christ as Jesus, symbolized as a fish, suffered under muddy water. Muddy water represents the murkiness of the sense appetites of a carnal mind. So Spirit suffers, is limited by, Its descent into matter and our ego's material appetites. (B)

The message of Easter is we can achieve the same unity with Spirit that Jesus demonstrated. We can achieve the same Christhood. His mortal body was transformed into an immortal body BEFORE the crucifixion. At the crucifixion, He proved that the human body can triumph over physical death. He proved that our physical bodies, once fully spiritualized, are not subject to physical limitations. (C)

The commonly quoted expression, *"Eloi, Eloi, l'mana Sabachtani,"* which means, *"My God, My God, Why hast Thou forsaken me?"* is a mistranslation. It does not square with the life and teachings of Jesus Christ. Unfortunately it appears in almost all standard Bible translations. This errant translation intentionally tries to put distance between Jesus and His God Nature. And it's implication is if God forsook Jesus, God will forsake us too! What Jesus really said, in the original Aramaic, was *"Eli, Eli, l'mana Shabakthani"* which means: *"My God, My God, It is for this purpose I have come"* or *"This is my destiny."* (B)

The rooster crowing to signal Peter's denials is an ancient symbol that represents the discordant vibrations within us that are set into motion when we deny our divine connection. An inner alarm sounds that registers in our conscience telling us to re-establish the body, mind, soul connection essential for spiritual growth. (B)

Ego

I recommend an "I" doctor for anyone neglecting to walk the spiritual path on practical, progressive, positive feet. (B)

The human ego is our conscious identification with physical form. It is a form of sleep that exists to help us cope with our decision to become physical beings. (C)

The ego tries to urbanize the natural spirituality of our human nature. It attempts to level our "mountains of higher consciousness." It tries to dam the flow of Spirit, and does its best to pour an ego-driven grid of error concepts and desires upon our inner landscape. Our human task is to subordinate a recalcitrant ego so we can express who we really are — the Christ at the point of us. (B)

Embedded Theology

The truth is, in order to understand the depth of the Infinite Presence we call God, we must forget much of the traditional stuff we have learned about God from embedded theology, because much of the traditional stuff (translations of scripture) is based on mistranslations of scripture and biases by the neglect to include legitimate writings which reveal a deeper understanding of Biblical and metaphysical truths. (B)

Most people really WANT to enrich their spiritual experience, but they allow embedded theology and the fear it brings to keep them from stepping out in faith. Take the leap, stretch beyond the confines of embedded beliefs, and know the Truth of expanded awareness of your Oneness! (C)

Enlightenment

The Christ as Jesus said: "Take my yoke upon you… and you will find rest." He wasn't talking about the kind of yoke that harnesses a beast of burden like an ox or mule. We believe He was referring to the yoke of willingness. He was saying "Be as willing as I am to surrender your human self to your Christ Self. Become as receptive to Spirit's tug as you can be, and you will find the rest — that is, the enlightenment, the happiness, the peace of mind, the confidence, the creativity, the health, the strength — you need to make every day a good day. (B)

As we learn to "Cross our heart and hope to SEE Truth" we cross out error and move one step closer to enlightenment. The road to enlightenment means standing 'in light of' the Truth of who we really are, spiritual beings who have chosen a human experience. (C)

The goal of every sage, every spiritual teacher, every shaman, every Truth seeker is to become enlightened. Since humankind first became conscious we have wanted to become more conscious, more aware, more knowing, more enlightened. (B)

Entrainment

Jesus the Christ totally entrained His human personality so that His human nature became one with His Christ Nature. He lived, moved, and had His being in at-one-ment with Spirit. His Godness was enthroned in His human physicality. He had absolutely transcended the illusion of any separation between His human beingness and His I-Am-ness. He recognized His indivisibleness as God expressing Godness at the point of His human Individuality. (B)

Error Thinking

Fear, doubt, reticence, denial, and other negative responses to outer appearances can limit our good when we choose to hold onto anything which we allow to separate us from our I-Am-ness. (B)

As we cross out error thinking, we begin to stand in the Truth of what we know, and see beyond the world of appearances regardless of how much the world (the media, other people, uncomfortable situations, new experiences) tempts us to focus on the appearance of things. (C)

No matter what you believe to the contrary — you can go from error to eros. (B)

Error thoughts are mental indigestion. They surface from a consciousness addicted to things that aren't good for you. (C)

Errors are the results of spiritual arrhythmias. (B)

Like the sculptor who chisels the rock or marble away until the masterpiece is revealed, we must chisel away error thinking, self-defeating habits and inclinations, and anything that is not truly us. (B)

We cannot eliminate error thinking merely because we have a basic knowledge of spiritual truths and feel we are tapping into our spiritual powers (disciples). Erasing error requires a disciplined habit of going into the Silence (prayer/meditation). (C)

We are all professional rationalizers when you think about it! We are really good at coming up with explanations to justify our behaviors or beliefs. But think about that word: rationalize. It is actually self-descriptive: Rational Lies! Rational in that they really sound good, and make sense! But Lies—because they are like a good coat of paint over a flood-damaged car. They create an illusion that keeps us stuck and prevents us from moving forward! (C)

When the secular velocity of materialistic choices trumps spiritual discernment, soul growth is usually slowed and blunted. The effects of discordant thinking and acting create incongruencies in body, mind, and soul which increase the speed of our inevitable collision with our own shallowness. We must slow our secular velocity enough to speed up our spirituality. (B)

One of the most powerful actions we can take for our spiritual growth is to take conscious control of our 'mind critters' like: fears, doubts, false beliefs and assumptions; negative thoughts and emotions—all the stuff that is debilitating and draining. They can overtake us as surely as those wildlife critters can take over our yards and our attics! BUT, we have the power to control them. All we have to do is stop feeding them! (C)

At some point in our spiritual unfoldment we will see each error thought as a materialistic burr, something to be removed immediately. (B)

See past missteps, failures, and mistakes as 'skin school' tuition, not indictments. (B)

Eternal Life

The life Jesus promised us is a life of endless possibility, vitality, expanded awareness, higher consciousness, invigoration, vibrant beingness. A life without restriction, worry, or limitation. A life of unbridled joy and happiness. A life without the need for constant error triage. A life of passport-free travel around the Multiverse and beyond. (B)

We don't have to wait for eternal life. We have it now. We just don't know what to do with it. (C)

Evil

Evil is a form of error. The only existence it has is what we give it. (C)

Evil is purely a human invention. Evil springs from our unenlightened error consciousness which worships materiality and form. When we get into the right relationship with Spirit, there is no evil. (B)

Evolution

Evolution is a 'stepped down' version of the Eternal Presence. It's the physical form of Spirit on its way 'back up' to its original spiritual essence. Evolution's prerequisite, involution, is Spirit's descent into what we call matter. Once Spirit is materialized It begins Its upward movement (evolution) to reclaim Its transcendent perfection. Both processes, involution and evolution, are complementary movements of Spirit. It would be more appropriate to say that 'evolution' is really 'reclamation.' It is dissipated, watered down wholeness returning to its original state. (B)

Experience

We all receive information at the rate of 500 billion bits per second. What really matters is the outformation — what we do with the information. Will we use it to express our Godness through our goodness, or our godlessness through fear, greed, or selfishness? (C)

Spirit is concerned with the vernacular of the heart of an experience, not the ego-burdened event itself. The acoustics of experience, any experience, tweaks us, prunes us, even prods us to honor the Truth of who we really are. It is the tone of our responses that determines the quality of our lives. We have an opportunity to learn from each experience. Each experience is a catalyst for growth. Experiences, then, are a very real form of compulsory education. (B)

Faith

Faith is knowing from deep within — where you know that you know that you know, and where you trust in the knowing. It is the knowing that allows you to simply turn the faucet knowing you will get water — to hit the switch knowing you will get light — to sit in the chair knowing it will support you. It is moving forward knowing Truth Principles never fail. (C)

Faith is a spiritual night light in the hallways of darkness. (B)

Many people seek external proof BEFORE they step out on faith. Here's the secret about faith-lifts. People usually don't act contrary to their faith. They act contrary to their profession of faith. (B)

Access to a faithlift is kind of like being in the ocean, caught in the current, and you feel like you are drowning! As you look around, all you see is the ocean, and there is no way to escape! You just know you are going to drown! However, imagine that there is a life preserver right behind you. It is there, ready and waiting for you to reach out and grab it! But if you don't see it — if you are unaware — then you can't use it; it is no help at all! Our faith is the same thing. We can build our dreams, our goals, our solutions to life issues on the shifting sands of the world of appearance, where the slightest storm can wipe them out — or we can build our dreams, strong and solid, on a foundation of faith! (C)

The most noticeable kind of faith-based spiritual growth is heart-to-head resuscitation. (B)

If we are faithFULL we can release anything and everything that blocks our greater good. (B)

How often have you heard the expression, "Fake it till you make it?" We believe this is one of the most dangerous "cute quotes" tossed around the New Age circuit. If you are faking anything, it is not coming from the heart and essence of who you are. Spiritual growth cannot be built on fakery. Instead of advocating faking it, Bil and I invite you to use the phrase we use: "Faith it till you make it!" (C)

Cher and I strongly encourage you, adamantly invite you, to lose faith in God. We're serious—lose faith in a God who is the product of your ego projections, fantasies, and materialistic wishes. Lose faith in a God who is nothing but a lucky charm. Lose faith in a *deus ex machina*, literally a "machine God." Lose faith in an anthropomorphic God in the sky. Lose faith in a goodie God who bestows good to some and withholds good from others. Lose faith in a God who punishes and condemns and judges. (B)

Faith is the ability to believe with confidence — to have conviction — to know that you know that you know! And what's interesting is that Faith (like all the powers) is always active in our lives. It is up to us whether we use our Faith power to affirm our fears, the negativity of a situation, the world of appearance — or whether we use it to affirm what is true at the level of Spirit. And whenever we find ourselves bogged down in the world of appearance, feeling tired, depressed, angry, alone, self-deprecating — that's a clue that we definitely need a Faith Lift! (C)

In Sanskrit, the word for faith is *shraddha*, which is akin to *cor*, "the heart," in Latin. Faith is more a quality of the heart than of the mind. It is the knowing of the heart that transcends the intellect. (B)

The Fall

The 'Fall' happens every time we purposefully choose to excel in self-ology and greed-ology. Its origins occurred when we, as highly evolved spiritual beings, decided to create a physical experience and produced time and space as we know it. The 'Fall' was the moment we concocted our separation from Spirit and it happened BEFORE we became physical beings. (B)

False Prophets

False prophets, asphyxiated with greed, are the blood ticks of religion. They graft falsehood onto partial truths, and purposefully prey on naïve seekers who hunger for the Truth. (B)

On this spiritual journey we call life, you are going to run into all kinds of Truth seeker 'tourist traps' designed to create within you an illusion of separation from Spirit. These 'traps' can be a manipulative guru; a materialistic teaching; a fear-based theology; a money-grabbing, New Thought paraphernalia toting salesperson. Just recognize them for what they are, so you can respond to them appropriately. (C)

Fasting

Fast from toxic thoughts, beliefs, and attitudes that create an illusion of separation between you and your Divinity! Bil and I believe that when we fast from anything that interferes with our conscious oneness with Spirit, we are filled with joy! In fact, we base our perspective on Matthew 6:16-18, when Jesus instructed: "When you fast, don't look all gloomy, so everyone knows you're fasting." In other words, if it's just a façade, the fasting means nothing! And there's no lasting impact from it. "But when you fast," Jesus said, "put oil on your head and wash your face, so that it will not be obvious to others that you are fasting." In other words, when we allow ourselves to experience the absolute joy of oneness, and allow our light to shine as a result of fasting from error thinking, we will be rewarded with the growing consciousness of Divine flow in our lives. (C)

From a spiritual perspective, Lent stands for a voluntary retreat from the world to prepare for our resurrection from false beliefs, error thinking, and the denial of our innate divinity. That perspective suggests there is only one kind of fasting: abstaining from error thoughts that dampen our awareness of our oneness with Spirit. The fasting Cher and I advocate during Lent is dieting from doubts, fasting from fear, dieting from believing we are unworthy, and eliminating the thinking that we are sinful by nature. (B)

Fate

The assertion that 'nothing happens by accident' implies that everything happens as it is supposed to happen. And what is supposed to happen is determined by fate, or karma, or God, or cosmic beings 'out there' who are in charge of micro-managing our earth experience. Cher and I invite you to 'get over' that way of thinking as soon as possible. It places your power, and self-determination, and your ability to be the captain of your fate outside of you. We are NOT here to be the products of an 'outside in' fear-based mythology. We are here to be the architects of an inside-out spiritual practice. (B)

The expression *what will be will be* is a cop out expression. It is based on the perception of a God in the sky who orchestrates what happens to us without our knowledge or consent. It is a phrase which suggests that outcomes are determined by something outside of us no matter what we do. The truth is what will be is what we will to be. The point of power is our will power. (B)

Fear

Someone once said that fear is 'false evidence appearing real.' From a spiritual point of view the 'false evidence' appearing as real comes from our unenlightened ego which is grounded in materiality. When we subordinate our human ego to our higher spiritual nature the acronym for fear changes to: **F**acing **E**very **A**ppearance **R**ealistically. (C)

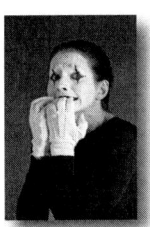

Sometimes life comes at you fast! That's what a TV commercial says. The advertisers are supposed to be selling insurance but they are really selling fear and uncertainty. On the other hand, Cher and I are selling assurance — not insurance — the assurance that we (you, humankind) can work all things together for good and that we (you, humankind) do not need to fear outer appearances. (B)

Here is a great formula for overcoming the paralyzing power of fear:
        F = Face It
        E = Embrace It
        A = Act Through It
        R = Reinforce Success (C)

Fear is one of the most insidious villains to take up living space in our minds. It was fear that kept Peter from acknowledging he was one of Jesus' disciples, leading him to deny Jesus three times; it was fear that sent the disciples into hiding after Jesus was crucified; and it is fear that keeps us from letting our lights shine, being the very best Christ we can be! Fear comes in many forms: fear of rejection; fear of criticism; fear of not fitting in; fear of failure; fear of pain; fear of isolation; fear, even, of success! In fact, fear can literally immobilize us! And it can stand between us and the awareness of the Oneness that is ours! So here's a great "Exit Line" for fear: *"My consciousness is greater than any fear I may encounter!"* (C)

First Coming

The First Coming is when Spirit descends into matter as the Christ in each of us at birth. God becomes incarnate in us, through us, as us! We are God expressing through the Christ at the point of us. (B)

Forgiveness

Forgiveness happens when we go from bitter to better. (C)

When we forgive, we release the need for a bitter past fueled by the erroneous belief in our separation from Spirit. (B)

Sow seeds of forgiveness and love. Release any and all grudges you are holding on to. Let them go. With forgiveness, you harvest the gold of a heart open to love, the gold of inner peace, the gold of deepened relationships. (C)

Forgiveness, it seems, is a universal human need. At its core it is the need to be pardoned, to be released from the emotional strain of having wronged someone or having been wronged by someone. In its literal essence it means going from bitter to better. Forgiveness requires an emotional correction. It is an empathic response to a wrong doing. It constitutes an act of extraordinary consideration which oftentimes seems much too lenient, if not down right foolish. But forgiveness is not doormat theology. Metaphysically, forgiveness means giving up the false for the true. Another way of saying that is it means giving up our fixation with fiction. The kind of fiction I'm referring to is our attachment to any falsehood which blocks our spiritual growth. (B)

As you recall bad treatment, grudges, or any other emotionally-laden event, pause in that moment and send a blessing to the people who were involved. Wish for them their highest and best. As a result, you will be blessed abundantly. (C)

So many illnesses have been connected to our emotions — and we carry grudges like badges of honor. Research has demonstrated that consistently carrying grudges can lead to stress, backaches, chest pains, migraine headaches, and even relationship and job-related problems. The message is loud and clear: holding on to grudges hurts the grudge carrier—not the person he/she is holding the grudge against. The saying "Forgive and Forget" is unrealistic! A wiser practice would be: "Forgive and Release!" (C)

We know we have truly forgiven when we no longer feel the need to tell the story! (C)

Four Horsemen of the Apocalypse

Much has been written about the Four Horsemen of the Apocalypse. Almost all of the interpretations center around external events which take place in the end times. Symbols of the 'Horsemen' include the anti-Christ, warfare, famine, plagues, and death. However, the Bible is the story of our evolving spiritual consciousness. So, like other people, places, and things mentioned in scripture, the Four Horsemen of the Apocalypse represent qualities within us. Although there are many levels of interpretation of those qualities, we see them as states of awareness: The white horse represents dogma that limits our spiritual growth and blinds us to greater truths. The red horse stands for the chemicalization that occurs when our old beliefs and assumptions are rocked by cognitive dissonance. Our thoughts war against each other as we try to grasp compelling spiritual insights. The black horse symbolizes our going through the 'dark night of the soul' as old beliefs and life patterns are challenged and then released. The pale horse represents the demise of our worldly, Adamic consciousness which does its best to resist the inevitable transformation which is occurring. (B)

Garden of Eden

In our own minds we "fell from grace." We forgot our omnipotent heirship and hid from our inheritance. We became afraid of the power we discovered. We had second thoughts about our Godness. We developed this neurotic idea that we are unworthy and undeserving. We feel shame and hide ourselves from our God essence — even today! We have unnecessarily — and tragically — derailed ourselves. We can reclaim our ever-present Eden, which is intrinsically expanding at the rate of our Christed awareness. And that reclamation begins with the realization that we are God indivisiblized at the point of us. When we open our eyes from that level of awareness, we will realize we have never left Eden — we only think we have. (B)

Genesis

We can turn the hardwired book of Genesis in the Old Testament into the neurogenesis of enlightenment. The term "neurogenesis" is the scientific term for the birth of new neurons. And the birth of new neurons strengthens the plasticity of the brain, which leads to expansiveness in our spiritual thinking, being, and doing. (B)

Giving

A spirit of giving comes from that place in you that recognizes you are connected with Divine Substance, and have access to all you ever need. Living from this spirit allows you to be generous in whatever ways you can. It's not about the amount you are able to give — it's about the attitude from which you are giving. Whether it's money, time, support, hope, joy — the underlying value is about your generous spirit. (C)

The act of giving itself is testimony to an awareness of the omnipresence of Universal Substance and our immediate access to that Substance. Giving vaporizes the veil of lack. (B)

Hold out your hands, palms up. Are you giving or receiving? It looks the same! Giving and receiving is a continuous cycle, each feeding the other. You cannot give without receiving; you cannot receive without giving. If you aren't involved in both, you are cutting off the flow as surely as if you put a kink in a hose. (C)

God

God is not a being having human qualities but the Beingness of Cosmic, Eternal, Principled, Universal Absoluteness. (B)

An external, anthropomorphic God 'out there' does not pull a new car off of a celestial parking lot and send it to us, or a diamond ring from a cosmic jewelry counter and see that we get it. God is not a goody God dispensing good to some and withholding good from others. (B)

GODISNOWHERE. This can be read as "God is Nowhere" or "God is Now Here." It depends on your perception ... and your perception will manifest in your experience! (C)

Every time we pray to an anthropomorphic God 'out there' we are perpetuating the false belief of our being separated from Spirit. We are disowning our true relationship with the Christ as us in human form. (B)

According to traditional translations God said, "Let there be light" and the universe began. God said, "Let us make humankind in our image." God said, "It is not good that man shall live alone." God said, "You shall have no other gods before me." God said, "I Am That I Am." These are some of the traditionally accepted versions of God speaking to the spiritual beings who were present at the 'beginning.' Unfortunately they reinforce the belief in an anthropomorphic God in the sky, a Diety which has human qualities, one of which seems to be the power of speech. (B)

We are the activity of God expressing in, as, and through us. There is no revelation higher than the realization that we are physical expressions of God being physical as us. (C)

Seeing God as the Sacred Unity, Cosmic Oneness, the Eternal Isness, the One Reality, gives us a more quantum view of God. It gives us a picture of the universality of the One Reality as the Source of all that is, both manifest and unmanifest. (B)

Because of the brain's neuroplasticity, a 'limbic God' turns out to be an oxymoron. (B)

God's Will

Humankind's conscious recognition that we are indivisiblized expressions of God at the point of us, and the disciplined actualization of our Christhood, are the will of God. (B)

The 'will' of God is Its 'isness' expressing Itself in endless forms and patterns in both manifest and unmanifest realms of being and non-being. (B)

Good Samaritan

The Good Samaritan story is about us. It is about our relationship with the Christ of us. It is about our falling in and out of a state of grace. It reminds us of our awesome and unfailing connection to Spirit. It encourages us to have Christed thoughts so we can make Christed choices. It prompts us to wear a mental WWCD bracelet which asks: What Would Christ Do? And it assures us that we shall be comforted. (B)

The metaphysical implications of the Good Samaritan parable are straightforward. When we choose to leave the peace and serenity of our spirituality (Jerusalem) and follow the temptations of our material sense consciousness (Jericho), we rob ourselves of our strength and vitality. Our error thoughts (robbers) can take us over dangerous emotional and physical ground, oftentimes resulting in life-threatening illnesses. Our wholeness will be restored when we are receptive to Christ-centered thoughts (the Inn) and accept the wisdom and encouragement that comes from our Christ Nature which gives us comfort through the Holy Spirit. (B)

Be a Good Samaritan by practicing sneak attacks of kindness. Do something nice for someone without being found out! Try doing it for someone you don't like so much! And every day remember to do something kind and loving for yourself! (C)

Gospels

The Gospels are 'how to' manuals for actualizing our Christ potential. They are filled with texts, tweets, and apps for unfolding our Christhood. (B)

Grace

We experience grace every time we think a Christed thought, have a Christed intention, make a Christed choice, and take a Christed action. Each time we choose we cause an effect and have an opportunity to get things right or make things right by re-causing (making another choice) our experience to produce a different effect. (B)

We are anchored in grace because it's part of our divine nature. (C)

We are 'grace full' expressions of Spirit. (B)

Gratitude

Cultivating a consistent consciousness of thanksgiving by becoming aware of the myriad opportunities to express your gratitude and praise is the essence of thanksliving. (C)

Be grateful every time you experience the acoustics of abundance. (B)

Gratefulness is the harmonics of a pure heart. (B)

We write "Gladly" on our checks (just above 'Pay to the Order of'). It helps us experience a sense of joy as we send our money out into the world. By allowing a sense of joy to flow through us, we can send that joy out to others through our thoughts and energy. (C)

Toast each day with an attitude of gratitude. (B)

Gratitude is kindness doubled. (C)

Don't let 'thank you's' go unsaid. (C)

Counting our blessings is giving latitude to our blessings. (C)

Gratitude is a total body, mind, and soul experience. It comes from that part of the brain — the anterior cingulate — that registers 'soul' experiences. So, when we walk along our favorite beaches and feel the sand under our feet and the breeze blowing through our hair, or drive along our favorite stretch of highway, or step out of our homes at night and admire the canopy of stars overhead, or enjoy our experience at an Easter sunrise service, our souls sing and our bodies are revitalized with streams of dopamine and serotonin, the biological gifts of gratitude. So you see, feeling gratitude on a regular basis heals us at a cellular level. Being grateful is not Pollyanna and it's not to be taken lightly. It's serotonin to our soul and dopamine for our life extension. (B)

Thanks-living unlocks the fullness of life. It turns what we have into enough. It turns tolerance into acceptance and confusion into clarity. It can turn a meal into a feast, a house into a home, and a stranger into a friend. Gratitude makes peace with the past, adds humility to the present, and underwrites our prosperity in the future. (B)

Guardian Angels

Bil and I both have guardian angels. It was our guardian angels that brought us together. (C)

Happiness

Happiness, Harmony and Hope aren't condiments; they're the main course in the banquet called life. (C)

Our unenlightened self sucks all the ice cream off the top of the cone, then looks inside the hollow cone of sensory experience for lasting happiness. Too many people believe the promises generated by a hype-savvy conscienceless media which tells them they'll never be happy unless they buy the latest products and services. 'Brochured' happiness isn't happiness at all. It's simply the 'hollow cone' of materialism. A better tact would be to acknowledge the Christ within so that our outer experience will not be a hollow experience. (B)

When happiness is absent, our human journey becomes a maddening and lamentable undertaking. Perhaps all of our suffering stems from a happiness eclipse. (B)

Suppressing happiness is one of the chief illnesses of our time. (C)

Politicians call for a 'pursuit of happiness.' Metaphysicians recommend the 'happiness of pursuit.' (B)

Nothing ages as well as happiness. (C)

Harmony

The harmonious relationship we invite you to get really, really, really serious about is the one between your human self and your Christ Self. (C)

'Thoughts held in mind producing after their kind' is about the harmonics in our thought universe. Adding Christed thought to Christed thought harmonizes every atom, cell, and molecule in our body, mind, and soul. (B)

Healing

Recognizing our innate divinity and honoring the divinity in others, thinking positive thoughts, adopting prayer and meditation as daily practices, showing compassion toward others, offering forgiveness, eating right and exercising — are all movements toward wholeness. They are acts of healing, efforts to entrain the human us toward the spiritual us. In a very real sense healing is wholing. (B)

A healing spirit inspires you to reach out to others with love and compassion. It may even be an actual hug. I recently read an article called, "The Rescuing Hug." The picture was what caught my attention: it is of two newborns lying together in an incubator, with one little baby's arm around the other. The article details the first week of life of a set of twins. Initially, each was in her respective incubator, and one was not expected to live. A hospital nurse fought against the hospital rules and placed the babies together in one incubator. When they were placed together, the healthier of the two threw an arm over her sister in an endearing embrace. The smaller baby's heart rate stabilized and her temperature rose to normal. They both survived and thrived! The hospital changed their policy after they saw the effect of putting the two girls together, and now they bed multiples together. (C)

If you fail to take care of your present body, forget about looking for someplace else to live. (B)

Mediocre self-care is a meteoric route to illness and dis-ease. (B)

In a climate ruled by the worship of medical technology and based on fear, people prefer the risks associated with medicines instead of seeking spiritual alignment with their Christ Natures. (B)

As amazing as it seems, people can live with a dis-ease they don't know they have, but can't live with the diagnosis. (C)

One of the best prescriptions for an ailment: a couple of good belly laughs, rest, and a powerful affirmative prayer. (C)

Most diagnoses are medical boundaries. They are the ego's medieval walled city, erected out of limitation and maintenanced by fear. (B)

Thoughtless drug therapies are spiritual lobotomies. They numb the immune system, blind cells at the molecular level, and alter a patient's thinking toward dependency instead of wholeness. (B)

Everything the nervous system, circulatory system, endocrine system, digestive system, and so on — is interconnected at a neuropeptide level. To separate body, mind, and soul in treating dis-ease is simply bad science. (B)

Blood cells that rush to a wound site and treat the wound with a clot are wonderful paramedics. (C)

The human body is its own pharmacy. (B)

Sometimes an illness reduces us to our fighting weight. (C)

For some people a balanced diet is a beer in one hand and a pizza in the other. (B)

Heaven

We don't have to die to go to heaven — or hell — because both are states of consciousness which define our 'now' experience. Heaven and hell are not 'places' we *go* to, they're 'places' we *grow* to in consciousness. (B)

Heaven is our default state of consciousness. All we have to do is surrender to our 'heaven-ness.' (C)

The original Greek word used for Heaven is *ouranos* which literally means expanding, widening, magnifying, maturing. So Heaven is a process. It's an adverb, not a noun. It's not a physical place. It's a state of consciousness. (B)

Heaven is living joyfully, confidently, faithfully, and lovingly at the speed of our Christ Consciousness. It is more than a state of mind, it is a state of grace. It is a state of conscious oneness with Spirit and it is available to us each-consecutive-moment of now. It is as close as our next thought, our next choice, our next breath, our next action. We grow to Heaven every time we elevate our consciousness and hold spiritual thoughts and intentions. And the best thing about Heaven is we don't have to die to get there because Heaven is a state of heightened consciousness. (B)

People who believe in a literal Heaven believe the streets 'up there' are really paved in gold. Is their desire to go to Heaven based on spiritual growth or gold fever? Is Heaven a form of gold rush? (B)

Hell

Apart from our error-filled judgments and belief that we are separated from Spirit, there is no hell. Hell is an attitudinal sarcophagus. It comes with a consciousness of separation topped off with faith deprivation. The more we entrench ourselves in the belief that we are separated from Spirit, the longer we will remain bivouacked in a hellish consciousness. (B)

Hell is not a geographical location ruled by a red-garbed being with horns, tail and pitchfork, where people scream in agony and are tortured endlessly in eternal flames. The notion of this kind of hell has been popular for centuries. If you happen to have been brought up in a traditional Christian home, chances are this kind of 'hell' was passed on to you at a very early age. If it was, and if it is still your dominant belief about hell, I invite you to suspend that belief as soon as possible. (C)

A consciousness fixated solely on material things and personal aggrandizements is a consciousness bivouacked in hell. (B)

The "hell" referred to in the Gospels represents the word *gehenna*, which was in a valley southwest of Jerusalem, where the refuse and filth of the city was burned. It was actually the city dump in Jesus' day; it was a smoky, smelly, gruesome place. Centuries earlier it was even a worse place! Certain idol-worshipping kings of Israel had practiced appalling religious rites in this same place, sacrificing children in the fires. The region was called the Valley of Hinnom, which means "groans and anguish." A perfect name for such a grisly site, don't you think? (B)

Holy City

The Holy City, the New Jerusalem, is not only a fully Christed personal consciousness, it will be the collective Christ Consciousness demonstrated and lived 'religiously' by everyone on the planet. When we reach that planet-wide spiritual azimuth, we will have fulfilled our purpose as a species. (B)

Holy Spirit

There is an Intrinsic Life Force that permeates all that is. It is the Eternal Presence animating Itself in the manifest and unmanifest realms of being. The Hindus call it 'kundalini.' The Japanese call it "ki", the Chinese "chi" and in Christianity, it is known as the 'Holy Spirit,' the Comforter (*parakletos*). Its highly-charged energies ascend and descend in our spinal cord (the alchemical serpent), depending on our level of enlightenment. The white heat of Spirit travels up and down our spinal cord through powerful energy centers (chakras), purifying, cleansing, and activating these spiritual transformers. I believe John 3:14 and 15, as well as other New Testament passages, refer to this kundalinic rise of serpentine energies: "[14.] And as Moses lifted up the serpent in the wilderness, even as the son of man be lifted up, [15.] That whosoever believeth in him should not perish but have eternal life." (B)

Hope

Lots of people scoff at hope — and they talk about "false hope." I believe there is no such thing as false hope! Someone can lie to you and you can lie to yourself; but hope is an awareness that is never false. Sometimes hope is the one thing that can keep someone going — and it can become the connecting link that moves that person from despair to an awareness of faith which can bring solutions, peace, and success. (C)

It is a natural tendency for us as evolving spiritual beings to be hopeologists. Hope, after all, is spiritualized wishing. It seems to be a necessary prerequisite for faith-lifts. (B)

Hope is patience that leaves the light on for you. (B)

Humankind

Humankind is one of God's 'skin school' addresses. To take our God essence out of the equation is strip-mining humanity. (B)

The term 'humankind' is our way of communicating the oneness of our collective individualness. We are putting everyone together, seeing the allness of our eachness, affirming the Divinity of every being. (C)

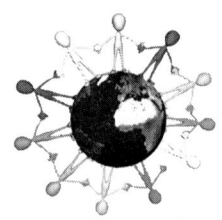

Identity

As you look at where you are in your life today, as you consider who you are and what you are, know that you are more than the sum of your parts — you know, parts like your talents, skills, heritage, physical image, mistakes, education, work history, financial portfolio, aspirations, choices. You are God expressing through the Christ as you. (B)

The new you isn't defined by old thought patterns. It's defined by your current awareness that they ARE old thought patterns. 'Error thoughts' are the products of lack consciousness. They are based on the false security of outer appearances. They have no power in and of themselves. (C)

We truly are Christs in the making. You may be thinking: *Bil, did you just call me a Christ in the making? Do you realize you're talking about me? I can hardly make ends meet. I'm not that smart. I don't make that much money. I'm not famous. You're putting me on too high of a pedestal.* You may want to fasten your seatbelt. I called you a Christ in the making because you are the Christ at the point of you. You may not be conscious of your divinity. That's what I mean by 'a Christ in the making.' (B)

I invite you to Christ up! View your life from your Christ perspective. Imagine how fulfilling and thrilling your life will be when you live at the speed of your Christ Consciousness! (B)

You've probably heard the expressions, "He/she's only human" or "It's human nature." It's generally used to excuse mistakes and poor choices. And it's based on the notion of our unworthiness and sinfulness, two terms used by those still stuck in pediatric theology. The truth is, we are divine by nature. The mistakes we make do not come from our true nature, they come from our human nurture, actually our lack of nurture. The mistakes we make come from our bruised, frightened, selfish, unenlightened egos. (B)

If you are wearing a mask of fear, or guilt, or unworthiness, or anger, or jealousy, or worry, or envy, or revenge, or greed, or hatred, or unforgiveness, or anxiety, or pride, or any other kind of self-diminishing mask — it's time to move beyond your *maskunfusion*. (B)

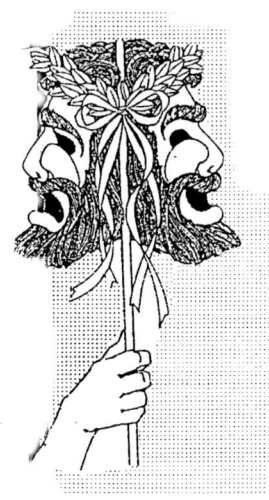

It is our brain, an organ we invented, that morphs together a multiplicity of moments that lead to a dynamic process of 'self-ing.' This willful act of blending moments into a homogenous whole is the mind's way of perpetuating the illusion of a self separate from the Self. (B)

"*Know thyself*" is an Ancient Greek aphorism. It is inscribed in the *pronaos* (forecourt) of the Temple of Apollo at Delphi. Its Latin equivalent: *temet nosce* means *"Thine own self thou must know."* Fifteen hundred years later William Shakespeare paraphrased the ancient dictum by reminding us: *"This above all — to thine own self be true."* Be true to what self? Our true Self, of course! Our Divine Self, our Christ Self! Our capital 'S' Self! The I Am Presence within us that works in, as, and through us. *"To thy Christ Self be true,"* Willy might have said. And then Willy says: *"And it must follow, as the night follows the day, thou canst not then be false to that self."* In other words we must walk our talk. We must be authentic. Real. Genuine. The product of the teachings we study. (B)

Illusion of Separation

Every time we pray to an anthropomorphic God 'out there' we are perpetuating the false belief of our being separated from Spirit. We are disowning our true relationship with the Christ as us in human form. When we do that we are blaspheming. (B)

The great lie that we've bought into, the lie that has gotten us into another human incarnation, is the deep-seated illusion of our separation from God. (C)

Immortality

We are already immortal beings — have been even before the Big Bang that created our universe. Our beingness is timeless and eternal because we are God's Presence expressing Itself as us. As we subordinate the personal ego, the particular 'garment' we wear in each incarnation, we will see our eternalness more clearly. (B)

Immaculate Conception

When our intuitive intelligence, love, and receptivity to our innate divinity are raised to their highest and purest spiritual essences, we immaculately conceive a pure, inviolate Christed Idea. (B)

Incarnation

Human incarnation is the pain body; it is a form of amnesia, a gauntlet of forgetting, the mindless denial of who we really are. (B)

Our incarnation is Spirit descending into matter as us. Each 'us' is an outpicturing of the 'us' before. (C)

Our incarnation is not a necessary condition for enlightenment. However, it is sufficient for our soul growth. (B)

We are both ancestor and heir, host and guest, to our continued spiritual growth. We are not only multi-storied spiritual beings, we are multi-dimensional quantum beings. (B)

Inconvenient Truth

Cher and I believe there will be peace on earth when people the world over have the courage to face the most inconvenient spiritual Truth of all time. It is amazing the lengths to which traditional Christianity has gone to downplay this universal Truth. The most inconvenient spiritual Truth of all time is this: The Only Begotten Son born in a manger to Joseph and Mary is the same Only Begotten Son born in each of us. The Only Begotten Son is the Christ Presence within us, expressing Itself in, as, and through us. (B)

Just because a Truth may be "inconvenient" and unpopular does not make it any less a Truth. We will experience incredible spiritual growth once we realize the power of embracing those "inconvenient" Truths with gusto! (C)

Indwelling Spirit

The Indwelling Spirit is our Inner-Net. (C)

We must express our innate divinity instead of suppressing it. We must let our Christ Light shine. Many people are sleeping like the disciples in the Garden of Gethsemane. The Christ is working within us to restore us to our Authentic Self. All we need to do is pay attention. (B)

You know when you are in sync with Spirit: doors open, resources appear, synchronicity happens, abundance comes, your energy heightens, you experience an abiding sense of inner peace, your health improves, and your happiness increases. (B)

Inner Peace

When we truly have inner peace, the acne of outer appearances will have little power over us. The clearer our inner vision, the clearer will be the face we show the world. (B)

The more at peace we are within, the better we can pick up the pieces without. (C)

Intelligent Design

The imprints of an Intelligent Designer are certainly compelling. The threads of traditional science and the dogma of pediatric theology are obviously wearing thin and are in need of triage. Their days are numbered. The narrow-minded nihilism of traditional science and the arrogant divisiveness of dogmatic religion have kept underlying universal truths hidden, ignored intelligent design, and have pushed us toward division and separation. Fortunately, there are a growing number of scientists from the fields of quantum physics, neuropsychology, neurotheology, astrophysics, and parapsychology who are collaborating with metaphysicians, mystics, and spiritual leaders throughout the world to pull us out of the dark ages. (B)

Intention Deficit Disorder

You've no doubt heard of ADD, Attention Deficit Disorder. I'd like to introduce you to Intention Deficit Disorder. IDD can block your spiritual understanding. And if it blocks your spiritual understanding it'll block your good. Intention Deficit Disorder is another way of saying unactualized intentions. Intentions, no matter how good or noble they are, never added a sliced onion to vegetable soup, or put a topping on ice-cream, or repaired an argument with a loved one. On the other hand, it is 'roll-up-your-sleeves, take action' intentions that bring us the results we want. (B)

Our very first action in our adventure toward overcoming Intention Deficit Disorder is to be absolutely certain we have set our intentions at the highest, most elevated level possible! So how do we do that? The best advice comes straight from the mouth of our great way-shower, Jesus as the Christ, when He said (in Matthew 6:33) *"Seek ye first the kingdom of God, and all these things shall be added unto you."* We must keep our intention focused on our awareness of our Oneness. There is no separation! Let no thoughts or worries that are inconsistent with Truth enter into our Consciousness. (C)

When we pay attention to our Intention, choose our higher level Intention over distraction, and Divinely declare our Intention from the most elevated level of understanding, we can transform Intention Deficit Disorder into Intention Divinely Declared — and walk the spiritual path on practical, Divinely-oriented, Understanding feet! (C)

Interfaith Traditions

We believe in freedom for people in matters of faith. The essence of spirituality, as well as religion, is a higher consciousness of God. We believe there are seeds of truth in all the world's religions. Different faith traditions are like spokes on a wheel, with the hub being God. They may be set apart by a variance of beliefs and approaches, different shades of theological interpretation, and a variety of rites and practices, but they are all seeking the One God (the One Presence, the One Reality, the Infinite Isness) at the center of all life. (B)

We believe that all spiritual/religious paths are valid expressions of honoring the Sacred. We honor all faith traditions to the degree that they do not injure others, infringe upon interfaith spiritual and religious rites and practices, or attempt to force their theology on others. (C)

We see immense value in interpreting Interfaith holy scripture metaphysically. In our ever-expanding openness to divine insights, revelations, and scholarship we believe metaphysical treatments of sacred literature bridge the gap between spirituality and religion, science and spirituality, and the physical world and consciousness. (B)

Irreconcilable Differences

When you hear the term "Irreconcilable Differences" you tend to think immediately of unsolvable disagreements between spouses, offering the technical grounds for a dissolution of marriage. When we use it from a spiritual perspective, it refers to two diametrically opposed beliefs in consciousness. Some people try to believe in Truth and error at the same time — and no one can do it! That's what Jesus meant when He said, "No one can serve two masters." We cannot stand firm in Truth when we are still vacillating on the effects of error thinking. (C)

Answered prayer and an unforgiving heart are irreconcilable. An anthropomorphic God in the sky mentality and metaphysical wisdom are irreconcilable. Attaining Christ Consciousness and lusting after material addictions are irreconcilable. Maintaining a white-knuckled grip on separation, duality, and dogma and an open-palmed approach to universal oneness are irreconcilable. Pronounced and arrogantly perpetuated warfare between the world's faith traditions and world peace and civility are irreconciliable. Mindless defense of literal interpretations of Biblical scripture and the acceptance of the heuristic value of metaphysical interpretations of the same scripture are irreconcilable. (B)

Jalopied Spirituality

Most literal Biblical interpretations turn out to be lower, more superficial, incarnations of religious exclusivism. They are a jalopied spirituality at best — limited to short trips into dogma and judgmentalness, but entirely unsuitable for longer, more open-minded excursions into the higher truths hidden within them. (B)

No matter how intellectually gifted we are, we must learn to listen to the wisdom of the heart if we want to be illumined spiritually. The wilderness referred to in most sacred scriptures represents the state of confusion caused by our dogmatic ego which keeps us from opening our heart to esoteric truths. (B)

Jerusalem Effect

The Jerusalem Effect is going inside into the field of peace and tranquility within us, becoming consciously one with our Christ Self. It's finding that inner peace in the midst of whatever is going on around us. (C)

Jesus

Jesus saved us from the illusion that we are separated from Spirit. He saved us from the absurd belief in an angry and vengeful white-bearded, white robed God in the sky. He saved us from the fantasy that we have to die to go to heaven — or hell. He saved us from the belief that we have to pay our karmic debts. He saved us from the self-deprecating belief that we are unworthy, no-good sinners. (B)

We believe in the divinity of the Christ as Jesus and we believe in the divinity of humanity. The spark of the Divine indwells in us and as us just as it did in, as, and through Jesus, though certainly not expressed to the same degree. We believe that the only way to God is through our Christ Consciousness. Jesus Christ showed the way. Jesus Christ became one with the Way. The Christ as Jesus doesn't have to be the great exception. He exemplified what we can become. (C)

As far as I know Jesus, the man, never wrote anything down. He never had a bestseller. Never wrote an autobiography. Never scribbled anything on an envelope. Had no use for a Mont Blanc pen. Never e-mailed, tweeted, or 'text-messaged' anyone! He did write something in the sand that no one knows to this day what He wrote except the church leaders for whom it was written. However, what he 'wrote' was a biography of the evolving spiritual consciousness of the human race — through His example. What He 'wrote' was our future through His Christed actions. What He 'wrote' was a roadmap of how we can align ourselves fully with our Christ Nature. (B)

Jesus did not say — "I came that you may experience lack and limitation, that your lives may be defined by poor health, and pimples, and cell phones that have dead zones." He said in John 10:10 — "I came that you may have life and have it more abundantly." (B)

When Jesus said: "I am the way, the Truth and the Life. No one comes to the Father except through me," He was referring to His Christ Nature, the I-Am of God individualized in human form as Him — and us! (B)

Jesus, the Christ, has opened the tomb of higher consciousness for all of us. He is the Roger Bannister of higher consciousness, the John Glenn of spiritual circumnavigation, the Neal Armstrong of taking a giant step for humankind. (B)

John 3:16

Metaphysically speaking, John 3:16 means: "The Eternal Isness, Absolute Good [God] manifests Itself [so loved] as the Cosmic Christ [Only Begotten Son] in human consciousness [the world], and whosoever comes into that Christed awareness [believeth] will move beyond the illusion of separation and duality [will not perish] and shall attain Christhood [eternal life]." (B)

John 8:12

In John 8:12, Jesus said, "I am the light of the world. Whoever follows me will never walk in darkness but will have the light of life." Metaphysically, light stands for awareness or wisdom. When we are connected with our Christ consciousness, we possess a wisdom that transcends the world of appearance. We know that we know that we know — and regardless of what negative situations we face (darkness), we have the answers within us and our wisdom guides us to the perfect solutions. When we have this awareness of our Christ connection, it shines out from us so strongly that others cannot help but be positively affected. They'll want to know how we do it! (C)

John 14:14

John 14:14 in its literal interpretation says, "Ask anything in my name, and I will do it." Its metaphysical equivalent means "Declare anything, affirm anything, intend anything from a higher spiritual understanding, from a consciousness of abundance, from an awareness that you can divinely order it — and you shall be able to materialize anything from the unmanifest into the manifest." (B)

Joy

Never miss an opportunity to sow joy. (C)

People who are bankrupt of joy or boycott joy are missing lifelong annuities of perpetual happiness, inner peace, and reverence for life. (B)

Work without joy is as hollow as an ice-cream cone. (C)

'Joy to the world' means bringing Christ-centered harmony (joy) to our human consciousness (world). (B)

If you aren't having fun in your work, you are paying too high a price. (C)

We miss out on a lot of joy in life simply because we won't try things we know we don't do well. Choose something you've always wanted to do, but were afraid to try ... and do it — just for the fun of it! Laugh a lot and fully experience the growth of stretching beyond your comfort zone. (C)

Judgment Day

Judgment Day is the day, in the end times, when we supposedly will all be taken before a God in the sky, who will render the final judgment as to whether we go "up" or "down." Is there an honest-to-goodness Judgment Day? You bet there is. But it's not where, what, or when most people think it is. Judgment day takes place each time we make a choice or take an action (set causes and effects into motion). If we are responsible for some wrong action of any kind, we are "punished" by the deed itself. Our thoughts and deeds are continually producing results either 'for' or 'against' us. No one escapes the Day of Judgment, because it is taking place every moment of our lives. (B)

Karma

Karmic Law is not the evidence of fate, but the movement of cause and effect. It is kudzu to the uninitiated, and a matter of choice to the wise who know they can re-cause their experience and avoid the negative effects of a karmic hangover. (B)

Karma is no respecter of persons. It is an equal opportunity reaper, an impartial judge and jury. (C)

Kindness

Both the giver and receiver of an act of kindness, as well as anyone who observes the act, experience an increase in their serotonin levels. Not only does serotonin make you feel good, but it also strengthens your immune system. It's amazing. Just by watching or hearing about someone doing something nice for another person, you improve your health and strengthen your own immune system. (C)

Kingdom of Heaven

Our innate divinity, the Kingdom of Heaven, is more than just in us — it's a deeper, more spiritual level *of* us. It is the Christ dimension of us, the somatic home of our Eternal Cosmic Self. (B)

The best way to narrow your focus is to spend some time at Headquarters. That's what we call the Kingdom of Heaven within us. That kind of internal focus should be your first response to any overwhelming problem. (C)

The Kingdom of Heaven is the vernacular of spiritually-charged ideas. (B)

How do we access the Kingdom of Heaven so we can experience the daily joy, inner peace, and prosperity that comes with living there? We don't have to guess at it. Jesus the Christ gave us the three keys to entering the Kingdom of Heaven in the first three sentences of the Lord's Prayer. (C)

Kingdom of God

The Christ as Jesus told us many times that his kingdom was not of this world. And 'the world' he was referring to is sense consciousness, the world of the unenlightened ego, and the limited perspective it brings with it. He also told us that in his Father's house are many mansions. His Father's house is the Kingdom of God or Christ Consciousness; and many mansions represent levels of expanded awareness and/or expanded beingness. So, in the Kingdom of God there are many states of expanded awareness and/or expanded beingness. (B)

Kundalini

The wattage of our interior kundalini fire depends on the amperage of our spiritual practice. (B)

Lack Consciousness

The word limitation has the words limit and imitation in it. It doesn't take a giant leap in insight to see that whenever we repeat (imitate) self-defeating thoughts and behavior, we limit what we can be. We limit our good because we limit our access to Spirit. (C)

There is a hydraulic relationship between lack consciousness and lack of opportunities. The greater our lack consciousness the fewer opportunities we will create. You would be surprised how people never miss an opportunity to miss an opportunity. The truth is opportunities don't come to us — they come through us! (B)

> *Bil and I don't believe in luck, any more than we believe in lack. We know that through our Consciousness and our power of choice, we create our experience in every moment. (C)*

Nothing can ever be taken from us that is ours by right of consciousness. (C)

Lack consciousness comes from an anesthetized awareness of the omnipresence of abundance. (B)

To transform a lack consciousness, try repeating this great denial/affirmation statement every day: I have now transcended all patterns of lack. I am rich and prosperous. Money flows to me easily and effortlessly, and I stand in the midst of the Divine flow of giving and receiving. I give thanks for ever increasing abundance in all areas of my life. I am a radiant expression of God as Divine Prosperity. (C)

Law of Mind Action

The Law of Mind Action is usually phrased 'a thought held in mind produces after its kind.' Produces what after its kind? Here's our take on what it produces. It does not produce material things. It produces more of the same kind of thoughts. And similar thoughts produce similar intentions, and similar intentions produce similar choices, and similar choices create behaviors consistent with the original thoughts which started the process. And those enlightened behaviors produce actions consistent with a spiritually attuned consciousness. (B)

Instead of practicing the Law of Mind Action many people succumb to the 'lull of mind action.' (B)

Light

No matter where you go, how you go, when you go, or why you go, God leaves the Light on for you. (B)

Are you traveling through life weighted down with fears, resentments, past self-defeating beliefs, grudges, what-if's, and material stuff that gets in the way of your spiritual growth? It's time to think about traveling light! Release anything that is not serving your highest good. Let it go! Give it away. Sell it. Travel light! I invite you to go a step further. Don't just travel light — Travel As Light! Be a beacon along the journey, so everyone who sees you will feel the energy of your Christ Consciousness and will themselves be lifted to a whole new spiritual octave! (C)

Instead of "This little light of mine," Bil and I prefer to say (and sing) "This Christ Light of mine." Be sure to let yours shine! (C)

One of humankind's chief tasks as spiritual beings in human form is to understand our true nature. We must declare our independence from error thinking, being, and doing. One of our chief responsibilities as beings of Light is to declare our independence from material appetites and the belief in duality and separation. We must declare once and for all our absolute independence from self-negating thoughts, assumptions of our unworthiness, and error-bleaching beliefs which spring from embedded theology. (B)

Genesis 1:14-19 says: "And God said, Let there be lights in the firmament of the heaven to divide the day from the night; and let them be for seasons, and for days, and years: ... and it was so. And God made two great lights; the greater light to rule the day, and the lesser light to rule the night...: and God saw that it was good. And the evening and the morning were the fourth day." Here we are talking about two great lights: the sun and the moon, which metaphysically represent the development of our spiritual understanding and the will to make the right choices. The seasons represent the different stages of unfoldment we experience as we gain higher levels of spiritual understanding. (C)

The Light of the World is the Christ Presence within our human consciousness. We are the Light of the World dressed up as us! We are divine beings having a 'skin school' experience. Within our being — within our body, mind, and soul — there is a Divine Presence which lights up our inner landscape. It guarantees the awakening of our human consciousness (the world). (B)

Literal Interpretations

Literal interpretations of scripture are religious tinnitus. They result in a feeling that there's 'something' useful 'in there' but all you hear is a dogmatic ringing in your ears. (B)

Now, literal interpretations of sacred scripture have their place, but when we find stories about burning bushes that talk to you, the Sun standing still, the Main Character of the New Testament walking on water, and water being turned into Manischewitz wine at a marriage in Cana we question the literal validity of these events. Our intuition — and common sense — tell us that bizarre literal interpretations are like pop up ads on Internet Home Pages telling us to look for deeper spiritual teachings associated with those accounts. (B)

When you stop with a literal interpretation of scripture, it is like eating the menu instead of the meal. You miss the real meat of the message — the practical lessons that can transform you at a soul level. (C)

Lord's Supper

Metaphysically speaking, the Lord's Supper symbolizes the conscious union between our human self and our Christ Self. A sort of spiritual alchemy takes place, as symbolized by the bread and wine. And it takes place in the Upper Room, which signifies a high state of spiritual consciousness. When we are in an 'Upper Room' state of consciousness, we have the wisdom to know the difference between sacred truths and falsehoods. We know the difference between the centrifugal force of materiality and the pull of Spirit. (B)

Love

Unconditional love is NOT permission to be used and abused! Using Jesus as our model, I think we can all agree He was not one to be a doormat! Talk about moxie — Jesus demonstrated it before the word existed! (C)

Choosing love over error works not because Cher and I say it works. It works because love is God's Isness in expression. It is the rock, the foundation, the eternal harmonics of our spiritual and human happiness. Love is the ultimate expression of our belief in our oneness with Spirit. It is the spiritual glue that unites us with the 7 billion expressions of it around the world. Love is the open sesame to the mastery of our human experience. Love is all there is. We just have to climb out from behind our error filters long enough to see it, feel it, and express it. (B)

Love is that harmonizing power that brings inner peace and divine connection wherever you are, regardless of the circumstance. So amp up your love ... the sweet, divine harmony of Spirit. (C)

Matthew 5:44 (NIV) says: "Love your enemies and pray for those who persecute you." Metaphysically speaking, Matthew 5:44 says: "We will deepen our Truth walks when we raise error thoughts (love our enemies) to spiritual thoughts. We do that by making a soul connection (pray) with Spirit which erases errors and attachments (those who persecute us). (B)

Unconditional love is seismic. It's the shortest distance between fundamental religions, New Thought schools, and eastern faith traditions. (B)

Whenever you are in a situation where you feel out of peace, out of divine harmony, tied up in emotional knots, use the KNOT to tie yourself together!

K = Know the Truth of who you are.
N = Nurture the situation and all involved through a blessing!
O = Own your power of choice.
T = Transcend the world of appearance!

This simple formula can quite literally transform your life! All you have to do is put it into practice, and BE LOVE. You will attract only the highest and best to yourself. (C)

Luke 18:18; 20-24

Luke 18:18; 20-24 is about a rich young man who gets a reality check from Jesus. While there's some truth to the literal interpretation of this story, it is grossly misleading. Worldly riches can, and often do, interfere with our spiritual growth. But that's not what the story is about. The literal version of the story implies that worldly things like: living in a nice home, driving a nice car, enjoying a golf or tennis membership, being well-portfolioed, wearing a respectful amount of bling, owning time shares, spending weekends at the beach or mountains — make it difficult for us to get to heaven.

Traditional churches and religious cults have used this scripture to raise funds and separate people from their money for hundreds of years. The idea is to make people — rich and poor alike — think that having material things is a barrier to getting into heaven. It's not things that keep us out of heaven; it's our attachments to those things that's the issue.

From a metaphysical perspective, this passage has nothing to do with physical things. It is not talking about liquidating our assets or giving all we have to the poor. It's about choosing spiritual inclinations over material ones (not bearing false witness). It's about staying true to spiritual Truths (not committing adultery). It's about applying eternal Truths that have stood the test of time (honoring our parents). It's about transforming materialistic thoughts and beliefs (the poor) into Christed thoughts and beliefs. (B)

Materialism

Since materialism is wrapped in horizontal consciousness, it will always be vertically challenged. (B)

Cher and I believe that possessing material possessions is okay as long as they don't possess us. Money and possessions are fine. We have a nice house and nice cars. I'm attracted to Cher, golf, metaphysics, and writing. Cher is attracted to me, ballroom dancing, crossword puzzles, and our Apple computer. The important thing is not to allow material things to hold you hostage. They're fine as long as they don't hold your health, happiness, and well-being as collateral. (B)

The world keeps telling us we have to have "stuff" to be happy ... and yet, it seems the more stuff we have, the more stuff we want! And the less happy it all makes us feel. What if we adopted the practice of releasing something every time we bought something new? What if we released any material thing we have not used or cherished in the last two years? Imagine how free we would feel! And we would be open to the spiritual gifts that could flow into our lives. (C)

Matthew 13:12

In Matthew 13:12 the Christ as Jesus says, "For whosoever has, to him shall be given, and he shall have more abundance: but whosoever has not, from him shall be taken away, even what he has." Doesn't seem fair, does it? Many people interpret that verse to mean that the 'rich get richer and the poor get poorer.' And they believe Jesus is affirming it. Here's Matt.13:12 from the metaphysical perspective: 'The rich (those who align their consciousness with their Christ Self) will manifest whatever they need for their spiritual growth and human happiness. But the poor (those who are attached to their material appetites) will lose many opportunities for enduring growth and happiness.'(B)

Meditation

Meditation is medication. (B)

Bil and I believe disciplined meditation is THE way to truly become consciously ONE with your Spiritual Center … your innate Divinity … your Christ Consciousness. (C)

Passive prayer and meditation will not produce an active Truth walk. (B)

The more you go into the Silence, the more you will live out loud. (C)

As it turns out, affirmative prayer and meditation are two of the highest forms of nutrition. (B)

Learn to make friends with your "monkey mind" and realize that taming that inner voice is all part of the meditation process. Don't fight it; thank it for sharing and direct it to be quiet. (C)

There is no 'one best way' or 'one right way' to meditate. All meditation techniques are simply strategies to develop your ability to focus . Once you have mastered that, you can enter the Silence. (C)

Metaphysical Malpractice

Metaphysical malpractice can become kudzu to an evolving spiritual practice, putting a coating of false assumptions on Truth that can be difficult to climb out from under. (B)

When you create guilt for someone by asking them what they did to cause their misfortune, you are committing metaphysical malpractice. (C)

The rate at which some people can engage in metaphysical malpractice is directly proportional to the embarrassment they can tolerate. (B)

Metaphysical malpractice is a trademark mistake made by those who dabble mindlessly in higher thought. And the worst thing is when we do it to ourselves! (C)

Metaphysics

Every once in a while repot yourself with new metaphysical and scientific perspectives so you don't grow stale. (B)

We define a metaphysical interpretation of ANYTHING to mean seeing people, places, things, and events that happen 'out there' as human and spiritual qualities, talents, and abilities — as well as faults — within us. (B)

Don't let the big word scare you! Metaphysics allows us to delve deeper into the understanding of the nature of God, and explore the Spiritual Truths that underlie and transcend all physical manifestation. (C)

Mental Kudzu

Kudzu is an insidious vine that can absolutely take over an area. In fact, it has been nicknamed the "foot-a-night vine," the "mile-a-minute vine," and "the vine that ate the South!" We have thoughts that do the same thing to us! They start out small, but they can quickly dominate our thinking. Grudges, resentments, hurts — if we let them have space — will soon clutter our mental landscape! Bil and I call this 'mental kudzu.' (C)

Mind Action

It's important to know the difference between mind action and mind auction. Mind action is based on purposeful thinking. Mind auction is doing mindless things like: allowing our busy schedule to push prayer and meditation off our schedule; slipping into old habits of doubt, fear, and weariness; reliving hurts caused by someone close to us without wanting to let them go; and allowing excuses to take the place of healthy life styles. (C)

Dogmatic thoughts are crude mental belches. (B)

People confuse the Law of Mind Action with a magic wand or a genie in a bottle. There is nothing magical about how it works. It's a systematic process of energizing every thought with another thought focused on what it is you desire, from an "essence" point of view. These energy thoughts attract Divine Ideas, which you then must put in action to manifest the outpicturing of your desires. (C)

Neuropsychologists are telling us that neurons which fire together wire together. These 'wired' neurons not only create new neural structures, their 'firing together' can actually leave lasting impressions on our brains — even from fleeting thoughts and feelings. So, what we think and feel are critically important for our health and wellbeing, and for our spiritual growth. We are not only the alchemists of our thoughts, we are the alchemists of our neural real estate and somatic well being. (B)

Wholesome, spiritually-charged changes in the brains of millions of people can tip the world in a more spiritual, peaceful, and caring direction. Join us today by adding your positive, spiritually-inspired thoughts to elevate humanity's collective consciousness. (C)

The neuroplasticity of metaphysical thought rewires spiritual perspectives and prunes the dogma from religion, synapse by synapse. (B)

It is metaphysical myelination, not religious literalism, that insulates us from the illusion of separation and duality. (B)

Our minds will accept the reports of our materially-addicted senses unless we over-ride its negative orientation. That's what the Hebrew Testament story in Numbers, Chapter 13 tells. Moses sent spies into Canaan asking them to report what they saw. The reports he received were negative and adamantly against entering Canaan, with the exception of two of the scouts (spies). This story is a treatise on the mind's "negativity bias." (C)

Mind action that perpetuates positive, spiritually attuned sentiments goes against our evolutionary template which has primed us for a 'negativity bias.' Mindfulness of our proper place in this human incarnation will keep us neurons above negativity. (B)

Miracles

Miracles are seen as probabilities and possibilities morphed into realities. They are really cosmic snapshots of higher metaphysical Truth principles at work and our inseparability from Spirit. (B)

From a deeper, more spiritual interpretation, miracles do not interrupt or overturn natural laws. They are the out-picturings of higher spiritual principles which only seem to be magically directed at a particular person who appears to be the beneficiary of a set of fortunate circumstances. (C)

Money

Money is a legitimate, energetic form of prosperity — but it's not the only form. (C)

You've no doubt heard the expression, "Money doesn't grow on trees." Well, actually — it does! Do you know how much a good hardwood tree sells for, or a towering pine tree, or a super-sized Christmas tree? There's money in those trees from a materialistic perspective. I'm going to suggest to you that money does indeed grow on a tree, the Tree of Knowledge. Embedded in the Tree of Knowledge are Truth principles, including the spiritual laws of abundance. Once you know the laws, and practice them faithfully, you will be able to attract and enjoy awesome prosperity and abundance in the form of health, happiness, divine ideas, wonderful relationships, inner peace, confidence, energy, and money. (B)

Do not be vague, apologetic, or hesitant about money unless you want money to be vague, apologetic, and hesitant about coming to you. Money is only one of the channels in which abundance flows to (and through) you. Once you align yourself with Spirit, all financial channels will be open to you and money will flow to you freely so that you will have plenty to share and plenty to spare. (C)

Do not feel obligated or resentful when you pay bills and meet financial commitments. Such thoughts and feelings only attract more financial obligations to be met resentfully. Instead, see the money used to pay the bills as an investment you are making to improve your prosperity. (B)

People are looking everywhere for stimulus packages and bail out programs, but I'll put my money on the Christ Presence within me. (C)

In the midst of experiencing an "ebb" rather than a "flow" continue to believe in your future prosperity. Focus on abundance rather than lack. Pay gladly to reduce your debt in any way you can. Forgive yourself if you feel badly about the debt you have incurred. Give thanks for your worth — and never, ever confuse your net worth with your self worth! (C)

Mt. Sinai

Metaphysically Mt. Sinai represents a highly-attuned and exalted state of spiritual consciousness. It symbolizes a heightened awareness of the Christ Presence within us. Mt. Sinai is in here (I'm pointing to my head). It is a spiritual state of consciousness, not a material waste of consciousness. The same thing can be said for three of the world's highest mountains: Mount Everest, Qogir (K2), and Kangchenjunga. Mountains are primordial symbols for high states of consciousness. (B)

Mysticism

The aim of most spiritual and religious faith traditions is union with God. The aim of awakened spiritual faith traditions is CONSCIOUS union with the God Presence expressing Itself as us. (C)

When we feel the brush of angel wings, it is our higher self coming into at-one-ment with our Greater Self, the Christ of us. Our spiritual scaffolding may surround our beingness, but it is determined and reverential mystical practices that draw us closer to oneness with that Inner Blueprint, the Perfect Pattern which links us to Spirit. There is no dessert as satisfying as a mystical moment. (B)

There's a mystic in all of us. All we have to do is demystify who we really are. (C)

Unfortunately, religion's exclusivity bias derails it from its mystical roots. Until and unless it gets back on track, religion's derailment will prevent it from reaching the station and status it deserves. (B)

Namaste

Behold the Christ in every person you see. You don't need to do anything outwardly special, just make the conscious decision to behold the Christ, the good, within them — whether it is your best friend, a loved one, the person who cuts you off on the beltline, the customer who becomes totally irrational, or the homeless person who is holding up a sign on the street corner. That conscious moment of beholding the Christ in that person will magnetize the oneness you both share with the Indwelling Christ. (C)

Negative Thinking

Bil and I encourage you to live a LINT-free life. LINT is an acronym. It stands for: Listless Impoverished Negative Thinking — and we want you to be free of it! (C)

Some people have Ph.D's in negativity. You probably know some of them. There are people who wear negativity like a badge of honor. Others wear it like a straight jacket and struggle to get themselves out of a negative disposition. Negativity comes from a consciousness grounded in lack, and fear, and anger, and hopelessness. Here's the thing. All of us have been exposed to negative environments. We've been told we're not good enough, that we're failures, that we can't do certain things or have certain things. And there's a part of us, that wounded child part of us, that says — what if they're right! Cher and I put a positive spin on that kind of malpractice by saying — negation is simply a choice you don't have to make. And you certainly don't have to allow it to form outposts in your consciousness. (B)

Negative, hurtful, judgmental thinking is corrosive. It's the kind of thinking that soils our consciousness and spoils our spiritual walk. In its lowest form negativity is simply whine-ology. (B)

People who have Ph.D's in negativity are peerless at consistently hitting the nail squarely on their thumbs. (B)

It's not a negativity bias that holds us back; it's giving into that negativity bias that keeps us imprisoned in error thinking. (C)

Neuro-Theology

Neuroscience has proven beyond a doubt that even fleeting thoughts and feelings can leave lasting impressions on our brain. When you add the amperage of the spoken word as a vocal expression of those thoughts and feelings you literally change the neural structure of the brain. Positive thoughts and affirmations are not only essential for spiritual growth but they are necessary ingredients for emotional and physical wellbeing and for rewiring the brain. (B)

Prayer, meditation, visualization, chants, mantras, repeating key words and phrases, and affirmations all serve as 'keystone species' in our evolving spirituality. Without them we couldn't restructure our neural circuitry to move us beyond what neuro-scientists call a built-in 'negativity bias' which keeps us on edge and fearful. (B)

We strengthen our neural circuits every time we think and speak positive, life-affirming thoughts and words. Shooting positive affirmations from the lip short-circuits the negativity bias and diffuses the power of negative experiences. (B)

Omnipresence, Omnipotence, Omniscience, Omni-activity

We are Omnipotent, Omnipresent, Omniscient, and Omni-active at our spiritual core because Absolute Good is particularized as us. (B)

The powerful concepts of Omnipresence, Omni-potence, Omniscience and Omni-activity have two incredible things in common. They all start with the syllable "OM" which stands for the Christ as us, the I AM Presence embodied as us. It signifies our indivisible connection with the God of our understanding. These four 'omni's' also have the "ni" in common. Ni is short for nihil which signifies nothing. So you see, there is nothing — No Thing — under heaven or earth that can separate us from the all knowing, everywhere present, all powerful, everywhere active nature of God expressing in, through, and as us! (B)

The power of all the "Omni's" is alive within each of us, because we are God expressing at the point of us. Everything that is the nature of God is also the nature of us. (C)

Oneness

We see other-ness from the context of duality and separation. We must rise, in consciousness, above the myths of separation and duality so we can grasp the significance of our oneness with one another and with the Christ as each of us. (B)

There is no geography in Spirit. (C)

When you are at one with your Christ nature, your entire life is filled with synchronous God moments! (C)

Not your past. Not your childhood experiences. Not your bad experiences. Not your most ingrained habits. Not your lost opportunities. Not the old tapes running through your head. Nothing —No Thing — can separate you from your Authentic Christ Nature except your disbelief in your Authentic Christ Nature. (B)

In order for there to be oneness, there are some irreconcilable differences that must be taken care of between people, and families, and countries. Between science and religion. Between religions. Between us and Spirit. Between our human self and our Christ Self. (C)

It is our hope as ministers that one day people the world over will be so unified, and will have reconciled any and all differences, and will experience such oneness that when someone cries, all of us will taste the salt. (B)

The part of us that is not subject to the laws of space and time is our consciousness. And it is our consciousness that rents the veil of separation and duality. (B)

It is a lot easier to conceptualize about oneness for the entire planet than it is to make peace with a neighbor whose dog dug up your flowers. And it is even tougher to align your inner Christ Self with your human self. (C)

Only Begotten Son

The Only-Begotten Son idea does not refer to human genetics. It's more like spiritual DNA, or even a Cosmic Zygote of sorts. It is the Christ Principle which is incarnated at the point of us. Unfortunately, until humankind realizes that the Christ as us is our core identity, the Only Begotten Son will remain the Only Forgotten Son. (B)

If you'll keep an open mind and use your dogma repellant, I'd like to offer you a different perspective on who the Only Begotten Son is as mentioned in the Bible. I believe the Only Begotten Son is the Christ Presence within each of us. It is the same Christ Presence that was in Jesus. It is the same Christ Presence that was in His disciples, in His mother Mary. It was even the same Christ Presence that was in Pontius Pilate and Herod. It is the same Christ Presence that is in you and me and in our children and grandchildren. It is the same Christ Presence that will be in the next child who is born. Snap yourself out of the illusion that you are mere flesh and blood. There is a treasure hidden within you — the Only Begotten Son, the Cosmic Christ which is expressing Itself as you. (B)

Optical Delusions

Many people are in a prison of sorts. They are incarcerated by optical delusions. Many people throttle back their consciousness by holding onto past beliefs and old scripts that keep them mired down in the shadows of rigid convention, religious dogma, and unhealthy assumptions. They live in a world of shadows, a world that gives power to outer appearances instead of inner transformation. (B)

When people act inappropriately, and disappoint us with their behaviors, it is important to remember we are experiencing an optical delusion. Look deeper and behold the Truth of who they are: worthy and Divine. (C)

Whenever we talk about "optical delusions," my mind immediately zeros in on magicians! I love watching magicians perform. A great magician is a master at creating "optical delusions." As Truth students and practitioners we can actually learn a lot from magicians. In a way, we need to be "reverse magicians." What I mean by that is instead of seeing a world of illusions, we see the Truth behind the illusions! (C)

Original Sin

The concept of original sin is a human invention that originated from Augustine's insecurities. It is a deliberate manipulative ploy to denigrate our innate divinity and create a 'curse' that falsely labels us as unworthy sinners. 'Sin' is an archery term. It means 'missing the mark (the bulls eye).' We miss the mark (sin) every time we deny our innate divinity. Cher and I believe in original blessing and not original sin. (B)

Pain

Pain is the price we pay for our no-holds-barred attachment to outer appearances. It is the soul languaging its disappointment at our longing for things which do not contribute to our spiritual growth. In that sense pain is our ally. It tells us we have missed the mark in our evolution toward fulfilling our Christ Nature. From a spiritual standpoint, when one person is in pain, we all have an interior hurt that must be healed. Pain is part of the human condition because we are asphyxiated on our supposed separation from Spirit. (B)

Everything is "pain-FULL" when we deny our divinity. (C)

Palm Sunday

The world of appearance can change in the twinkling of an eye. If we allow what's going on "out there" to define us, or get sucked into the negativity, or the excitement, we can become emotionally upset, confused, and frustrated. Our job is to wave the palm branches signifying the strength of our spiritual conviction, standing firm in our Truth. That way, we can move through any situation with grace, dignity, and peace — regardless of outer appearances or internal ego-talk. (C)

Metaphysically speaking, Palm Sunday represents our conscious surrender to our Christ Nature. It represents the reawakening of our childlike faith. Initially, this 'depth charge' of enlightenment stirs the entire consciousness (city in turmoil) and we sense there is something wonderful at work, but do not yet quite understand the full implications. This 'explosion of inner quickening' intensifies and leads to the process of inner transformation and cleansing. That's what Jesus' driving the moneychangers out of the temple means from an esoteric perspective. (B)

We want you to remember that Palm Sunday is about more than Jesus' journey into Jerusalem — it represents our conscious choice to be more spiritual ... to 'Be Still and Know' ... to stand in our Truth and show up as the best Christ we can be! (C)

Peace

In its broader, more metaphysical meaning, Jerusalem stands for 'the field of peace and tranquility within us that is the holy sanctuary for our Christ Self.' Entry into Jerusalem represents our conscious decision to commit to the eternal, indestructible, universal energies of our Christ Nature. When we become one with that field of peace and tranquility by entering the metaphysical Jerusalem conscious of our divinity we experience the Jerusalem Effect. (C)

When things pile up and life seems overwhelming, allow yourself the luxury of a few moments of meditation, breathing, relaxation — time to call forth your Divine Powers to open channels of guidance and peace. It is amazing how helpful 15-20 minutes of meditation can be in the midst of a chaotic situation. (C)

The search for peace implies we have to go somewhere. Peace does not come to us, it comes through us. (B)

Peace Be Still

We are password protected because we have immediate assess to the greatest security system in the world: the still small voice. And the password is: Peace be still. (B)

Be still and know that within you is the very center of your beingness, the Divinity that is the very nature of God expressing. The only way to really benefit from the awareness of your Oneness is to hit Pause for a moment and whisper: Peace, Be Still! (C)

Pediatric Theology

Literalists are products of what Cher and I call pediatric theology. They remain focused on the teachings from childhood religion, and need to move up to the next level of understanding: Spirituality and Metaphysics. (B)

Pentecost

Metaphysically, Pentecost occurs every time we express our highest and best spiritual nature in service to others. As we open up to Spirit, the fiery white heat of our inner Light shines. Our five senses are raised to their highest spiritual essences so that our Earth experience is filtered through the eyes, ears, smell, taste, and touch of an enlightened being who has deepened his/her understanding of Eternal Truths. Pentecost is more process than event. More internal combustion than external commotion. (B)

Perceived Obstacles

Obstacles are teaching points. Your challenge, as a student of Truth, is to determine if the "obstacle" means you are to reexamine your current direction or change course. It could mean you need to develop persistence, patience and skills on your current path. The "obstacle" could also be protecting you from yourself — to keep you from pursuing something that is not in alignment with your purpose. Knowing when to push ahead and when to redirect your talents and energies comes from experience and self-awareness. (C)

There is nothing more frustrating when you are traveling than to come to a sign that says "Detour for Roadwork." You want to scream "NO!" But think about it for a minute: aren't you really grateful for the warning? What if there was no sign? Imagine running off a bridge that was washed out, or hitting a road that suddenly ends because of construction? When you shift your perspective, you really are grateful for the warnings! And wouldn't it be nice if we had nice big warning signs posted for our spiritual journey, giving us a heads-up when we are approaching situations for repair? What if you saw a big painted sign saying, "Be aware you are about to have your belief system challenged!" Or maybe a voice comes over a loud speaker that says, "You are now experiencing the consequences of your false assumptions!" The moment we lose our focus of our connection with Spirit, we become entrenched in the world of appearance, and we feel ourselves facing ground under repair. It may manifest as fear, despair, loneliness, anger, doubt, self-pity, or any of a hundred other possible emotions. Each is a blueprint for separation — or an opportunity for some 'ground under repair' spiritual practice! (C)

Personality

God essence shines through the crystal prism of humankind and emerges as the component expression of rainbow colors manifested through human personalities. Our Christ Self, our individuality, is enthroned in physicality as our Authentic Self in our human personality. The result is one Source, many expressions. (B)

Philosopher's Stone

The *lapis philosophorum* is a legendary substance, supposedly capable of turning base metals into gold. It is believed to be the elixir of life, responsible for rejuvenation, enlightenment, and even immortality. It is better known as the Philosopher's Stone. The Philosopher's Stone appears in the Graal stories of King Arthur, and in thousands of other immortality stories all over the world. More recently it has appeared in the Harry Potter series of books. Cher and I believe the Philosopher's Stone, like the Holy Grail legends, externalizes an interior power we all have in common. We believe the Philosopher's Stone, like the Holy Grail, is not something material. It is not a physical rock, gem, jewel, or cup. It is not something we can use for selfish gain or material wealth. The Philosopher's Stone is the Christ Presence within each of us, the Christ Presence that expresses Itself in, as, and through us. (B)

Practicing the Presence

When we live, move and have our being from our Christ Consciousness, we are in the flow of life because we are practicing the Presence of God. (C)

Most people are herded by their secular activities instead of being heralded by their spiritual ones. They have allowed Good Morning America, The Today Show, and drive time radio to occupy the time slot once reserved for morning affirmative prayers and centering affirmations. Late night TV hosts help news junkies and entertainment groupies say their "amens" to busy, tiresome, and generally unfulfilling days. Giving prayer and meditation back their "time slots" so we can "practice the Presence" will connect us with the Spirit of us and bookend each day with an awareness that we are one with the Abiding Presence at the point of us. (B)

You become truly grounded in Spirit by spending time in the Silence. You'll find that by spending time in the Silence, you begin getting messages, insights, ideas, strength, wisdom, things you need. By giving time to Spirit, you gain a life of spiritual growth, inner peace, and pure joy. (C)

The Christ Presence as me is my 'habit.' (B)

If we neglect to 'practice the Presence' we can get knocked out of position by those off-road experiences and potholes we face in life: appearances of lack, illness, bad stuff that happens. And it becomes easy to get into a spiraling consciousness of negativity and doubt. It can happen before we know it. It's critical to constantly go to Headquarters, the Kingdom of Heaven within, and check our connection with Spirit to be sure we haven't been knocked off center. (C)

Live from a place of love in your heart. It can take on many outward expressions. When you live life from a healing spirit, you are always willing to give the other person a benefit of a doubt. You reach out in reconciliation, and allow yourself to be the first one to apologize. Forgiveness is a part of your way of life, and you behold the Christ in everyone. (C)

Every spiritual thought we have, every spiritual choice we make, every spiritual action we take is a pardon. A pardon from what? A pardon from error. A parole from the limitations of a warped ego. A pardon from suffering, lack, and limitation. A pardon from the illusion of separation and duality. (B)

You can have the perfect recipe — and even have all the ingredients lined up! But you can't eat the recipe! In the same way, you can know Truth principles and have them written down, but you can't 'eat the recipe.' You've got to apply the Truth principles you know. (C)

There is compelling evidence that Truth seekers who take the initiative in connecting with their Christ Center feel more confident and empowered, enjoy more enriched and productive lives, handle human challenges more confidently and expertly, meet health challenges more authoritatively and positively, and in many ways, are able to accelerate their enlightenment. (B)

You must release the notion that you can experience your Christ Connection just by reading, talking, or hearing about it. You must be willing to APPLY the teachings. Anything short of disciplined application is merely rhetoric. (B)

Prayer

There are no secret handshakes, passwords, or hoops to reach God — all you have to do is go into the Silence. Prayer has been the safety net for our business. It is the spiritual compass for our decisions. It is the key to our abundance and prosperity. (C)

Prayer is a spiritual Self-hug. (B)

Live a prayer-conditioned life. You can "pre-prayer" each day by praying in each day. This will keep you "prayed-up" so you are ready for whatever each day holds. (C)

Prayer is a way of life, a way to move through life with peace in our hearts. Prayer is a tool which we use to build our awareness of God within and to bring ourselves consciously closer to God. And it is this awareness of God's presence that keeps us poised and centered in times of challenge. (C)

The peoples of the world will be a lot better off when they stop *preying* on each other and start *praying* for each other. (C)

Prayer is not an activity we do to a 'God out there' or a ritual we perform to please an external deity. It is a deeply interpersonal experience in which we connect with our own God-potential. So, we do not really pray to God, rather we pray from a consciousness of our oneness with God within us. It is communion with that part of us which is the presence of God indivisiblized as us. (B)

It is through the acupuncture of prayer that we find peace and rest and answers. Bil and I invite you not to pray TO God, because praying to something or someone places God outside of us. It stems from a belief in separation. And there is no separation between us and our divine nature. The moment we stop praying to an external Diety and pray FROM the awareness of our oneness with our Indwelling Christ, we will accelerate the answers we seek. (C)

Although the methods of prayer differ, most people have been taught by the faith traditions in which they grew up to ask, to petition, to beg an external anthropomorphic deity in the sky for something they believe they don't have. They believe in 'dial-up' prayer instead of instant, high speed access prayer. When we pray FROM this unobstructed oneness, this indivisible connection with the Christ within, the good we want comes through us. It is FROM this inner place of alignment with the Allness of God that we position ourselves to receive. (B)

'Being careful for what you pray for' is fear-based theology. It is not useful to build guilt, and fear, and anxiety into a prayer experience. What is useful is to live a prayer-conditioned life, one which is characterized by absolute trust in your connection with Spirit. (B)

We can turn awful into awe-full using the power of prayer. (C)

Prayer is the world's number one antiperspirant. (B)

The best analogy I can think of, to help you recognize the power of a strong prayer practice, is to look at the difference between the old dial-up connection to the Internet versus having a high speed digital connection that keeps you connected all the time! Never underestimate the power of affirmative prayer, no matter how difficult a situation you are facing. Prayer works. That's my story and I'm sticking to it! (C)

Present Moments

Become a now-ologist. Live each-consecutive-moment-of-now from your Christ Consciousness. (B)

Our point of power is always in the present moment. The only thing that is important, the only thing that matters, the only thing that can help you master your human experience is what you do in this now moment. (B)

Prosperity

We are prosperous when we live joyfully, faithfully, confidently, and lovingly at the speed of our Christ Consciousness. (B)

No one can ever take what is yours by right of Consciousness! (C)

Many prosperity teachers shout, "Just hold the right thought and you can get (attract, magnetize) anything you want." Their theme is get, get, get. True prosperity is holding the right thought so you can GIVE, GIVE, GIVE anything you want! (C)

> *Whenever we experience lack of any kind, whether it's a need for employment, health, money, guidance, rest, etc., SOMETHING IS BLOCKING THE FLOW. We instinctively say, "Something's got to give!" And that insight comes from something deep within us that says, "You're absolutely right! Something's got to give and that something is you!" (B)*

What if we could live in a constant flow of prosperity, with the consciousness that there is always plenty, always abundance, never lack or limitation. Just imagine what that would feel like! We can do it! We really can! It begins with a consciousness of giving — giving from where you are — RIGHT NOW! It starts now, by getting into the spiritual practice of giving! (C)

When we move out of a lack consciousness, a fear orientation, a guilt predisposition, an unforgiveness mode — and into a consciousness of plenty, we will enjoy incredible health, wealth, and happiness. (B)

When we get into difficulty, it is so easy to focus on lack, to center our attention on the problem, to worry about blockages. But Jesus demonstrated that it is more important to focus on the potential. (C)

Economize your thoughts. Fill your mental bank with positive, spiritually-oriented thoughts and intentions. Delete negative, error-prone thinking from your thought universe. As you build your prosperity consciousness, there are things you need to let go of, attitudes you need to grow out of, beliefs you need to compost, assumptions you need to re-cycle. (B)

What you think often enough, what you say often enough, and what you do often enough determine the degree of success and happiness you will enjoy. (B)

We should not concern ourselves about unmanifested good. Right thoughts and actions help move possibilities into probabilities and hidden potentials into physical realities. When we're aligned with Spirit, we can "order up" the divine ideas, intuitive guidance, and resources we need for our spiritual highest and best, to move through life with grace, inner peace, and joy. (C)

There are no limitations — only a consciousness of limitation. There is no lack — only a consciousness of lack. Lackology and limitology are human inventions. Here's the truth about lack and limitation: they exist because we want them to exist. (B)

It is a myth that we must magnetize our good to us. The truth is our good is already here. We don't magnetize our good to us! Our good doesn't come to us; it comes through us. That is the proper directionality. Our job is to align ourselves with the good that is already here. The better we get at that, the more good we will manifest. The distance between us and our good is an illusion. And the illusion is based on the faulty belief system we have bought into. (B)

Let go of your good for your GREATER good! Sometimes we get so caught up in what we have — because it's so good — that we blind ourselves to something even better! We keep ourselves in a Spiritual Box, and get stuck there. (C)

Filling your consciousness with more prayer, meditation, and positive affirmations is prosperity shaping. It will get you past the 'LULL' of attraction. It will take you past the 'LULL' between manifesting something and waiting for what you want to manifest. (B)

Here's what we've learned about demonstrating prosperity. We can affirm all we want, storyboard all we want, visualize all we want, pray and meditate 24-7, and act as if the objects of our desires are already here, BUT, if we put our human self ahead of our Christ Nature, fail to forgive, or neglect our giving consciousness, we dam up the flow. (B)

Proverbs 6:6

According to most Bible scholars, King Solomon was considered to be the wisest man in Bible. So, it might seem a little strange for this wisest of the wise to tell us that if we want to become wise we should study ants. He tells us that in Proverbs 6:6. Here's the connection with the ant. Solomon was more than likely well versed in the wisdom traditions of the East and what we call the Mid-East. He was well aware of what the Egyptians called the *arat* and the Hindus called the *ajna*. Taoists call it the Third Eye. It's located slightly above the eyebrows in the middle of the forehead. When the Third Eye becomes active, one feels a tingling behind the skin of the forehead. Some esoteric traditions call that sensation "the tickling of the ant." So, in the Bible, when Solomon advises people to learn the ways of the ant and become wise, the ant's "wisdom" is a play on the esoteric 'tickling of the ant' when the 'clear sight' chakra becomes active. What Solomon is really saying is 'go inside.' If you want to be wise, "listen to the ant's speech" — that is, listen to your inner guidance. If you still think Solomon lowered his ear to an anthill to listen to ants, we need to have a talk. (B)

Proverbs 23:7

The books *As a Man Thinketh* by James Allen and *As a Woman Thinketh* by Dorothy Hulst are based on Proverbs 23:7, *"As (we) think in our hearts, so are we."* People find it curious that the languaging of Proverbs 23:7 seems so metaphysical. As we 'think in our hearts,' the writer of Proverbs reminds us. Think in our hearts? How can we think in our hearts? It may come as a surprise to some of you, but that's where our higher understanding comes. The heart is the wisdom center. It is the center of our intuitive intelligence. It contains the key to harvesting God moments because it is the stargate to the Christ Presence within us. (B)

Questions

Spiritual evolvement is less about unanswered questions, and more about unquestioned answers. (B)

Never be afraid to ask a question. It is better to feel stupid for five seconds while you ask a question than to be in the dark the rest of your life because you never asked. (C)

When you find yourself experiencing a difficult situation, instead of asking "Why did this happen to me?" one of the best questions you can ever ask yourself is: "How can I use this for good?" (C)

We have a great saying that has helped us innumerable times in our lives: Don't suffer from a pain in the ASK!" (B)

Rainbow

The rainbow is mentioned twice in the Bible: in the first book (Genesis 9:13-14), and in the last book (Revelation 4:3; 10:1). In the literal account of Genesis, God promises Noah that He will never flood the earth again. He tells Noah that He is placing a rainbow in the sky as a permanent sign of His covenant with humankind. The Revelation account refers back to the Genesis story. Metaphysically, a rainbow represents our etherealized spiritual power centers (chakras, astrological centers, the seven levels of consciousness, the 'many mansions' the Christ as Jesus referred to, the Twelve Powers, etc.) that must be quickened for us to master the human experience. The 'pot of gold' at the end of the rainbow is the Indwelling Christ. (B)

Red Sea

The Red Sea is our blood! Imagine the universal catharsis when every human being on the planet realizes that we are spiritual beings being human — that we can eliminate wars, and hunger, and sickness, and greed, and suffering. The most radical, pervasive, and earth-shaking transformation will occur when humankind truly evolves into a mature, rational, and loving species, which freely affirms and honors the Christ Presence within everyone. When that happens everyone the world over will be saying the same thing, "We have mastered the Red Sea." That is to say, we have mastered the earth experience. (B)

Reincarnation

Reincarnation is not a necessary condition for our spiritual growth. It is a skin school experience we choose because we still believe in separation and duality. What makes the skin school experience such a magnet is our attachments to materiality. (B)

Each reincarnation experience is our chance to matriculate through the illusions we spin. (C)

Our bodies are not only our biological addresses. They work quite well as our somatic space suits as we work toward erasing the illusion of our separateness from Spirit. (B)

Our repeated physical rebirths will continue until we outgrow our attachments to bling, flings, and things. (C)

Reincarnation is only one of the portals we choose to experience human form. Another choice is incarnation from another dimension of being. When we reincarnate, we've more than likely been here before — probably many times before. When we incarnate, we come here for the first time from another dimension of being in the Multiverse. Whether we're here through reincarnation (reembodiment) or incarnation (embodiment), the answer is the same: we've chosen physicality and its limitations over universality and its endless foreverness. (B)

Reincarnations are reiterations of our not getting it. (B)

Religion

Religious parochialism, prejudice, and pedestaled paradigms perpetuate the myth that one religion is better than another. The sooner we leave that childishness behind the better off we'll all be. (B)

Lots of failed churches confuse poor leadership, blunted church growth, and missed opportunities with Divine Order. (C)

Religion cut off from its mystical roots becomes sterile, myopic, and egotistical. It morphs into an instrument of elitism, judgmentalness, and arrogance. (B)

Religions are the thorns on the stems of roses, making the journey toward enlightenment (the flower) more difficult to reach because of their dogmatic snares and judgmental barbs. (B)

My hope is that religion will move beyond the embedded theology, prejudice, and exclusivism which divides people and that it will honor all faith traditions as legitimate paths to our awareness of our Oness. (B)

There is no such thing as a Lutheran sun, or a Taoist moon, a Jewish ocean, or a Roman Catholic forest, a Baptist sunrise, or a Buddhist river, a Muslim dessert, or a Methodist heaven. When humankind discovers this truth, we will have learned a way out of the religious myopia that is boring our youth, driving millions of people from churches, and dividing families and nations! (B)

The world does not need another religious denomination. (B)

I'm going to take a step back and say the future and relevance of religion depends on it becoming more spiritual and less dogmatic. And I'm going to take two steps forward and say the future and relevance of Unity, and other New Thought faith traditions, as a viable spiritual education movement is not trying to fit into existing religious molds or to justify its legitimacy by watering down its theology. (B)

When you lose your tolerance for other faith traditions, you've lost your footing. You've fallen into the same trap of judgmentalness.(C)

Religions that feed the amygdala are starving the anterior cingulate and deflating the frontal lobe, creating an anthropomorphic, vengeful, punitive God 'out there.' (B)

Research has shown that our nation's young people, and a growing number of adults, see today's Christian churches as judgmental, hypocritical, bigoted, Jurassic, politically motivated, sexist, disparaging toward same-sexed couples, and generally out of touch with reality. Clearly, mainstream Christianity must put away its childish things. (B)

Fear-based faith traditions reinforce what neuroscientists call the brain's evolutionary "negativity bias," keeping our 'flight or fight' response alive and well. Brain-scan studies have shown that fear produces anxiety, depression, neurotic behavior, high blood pressure, and poorer health overall. So, it seems as if fear-based faith traditions can be hazardous to our health. (B)

Research shows that a growing number of educated, open-minded, commonsensical people are unwilling to limit their spiritual growth by subscribing to any one religious belief system. From our perspective Cher and I have to say we applaud that cosmopolitan orientation. As Unity ministers we subscribe to Unity theosophy AND incorporate a multitude of 'best practices' from many of the world's faith traditions and scientific research to enliven and amplify our own spiritual practice. There's growth and enlightenment in inclusivity. (B)

Shall we cling white-knuckled to stale theologies or loosen our dependence on religious perspectives which dampen our Christ Light? (B)

Spirituality is religion — all grown up. (C)

Religious Victrolas

It is important for our spiritual growth to choose to move beyond memorizing and repeating literal interpretations of scripture. Otherwise, we may become dogmatic, religious victrolas, moving our lips without having been moved in our hearts. Just like a CD or cassette plays recordings of sacred writings without understanding their meaning, many people who settle for superficial religiosity are unaware of the scriptural passage's deeper Truths. (B)

Rest

Rest, metaphysically considered, is abstaining from worldly thoughts and intentions. It's having a spiritual moment. It's sequestering ourselves from any sense of separation and duality. (B)

Rest is a form of self-care. As spiritual beings having this human experience, we find ourselves inhabiting an amazing body temple. Our job is to take care of it. This means not only keeping it in good working order, but keeping our emotional being aligned and at peace, and doing things to ensure we are functioning from our highest, most effective level of Consciousness. And a key part of that is simple self-care. Every single day, take some block of time (from a minimum of 15 minutes to a maximum of the whole day) and do something just for yourself! Take a walk; read a book; listen to great music; dance; see a movie; draw a picture; go sailing; ride a bike; take a bubble bath; sing; take a nap; eat at a new restaurant. You get the idea! At the beginning of each week, commit on your calendar for X amount of time each day that is your time for you. (C)

When the soul's habitat abides in Spirit, there is sacred rest because there is a divine coupling. We must offer the soul the cradle it deserves. And that cradle is resting from error thoughts. (B)

Resurrection

Metaphysically speaking, no matter how dulled, deadened, or comatose we become (that's what Jairus' daughter, the widow of Nain's son, and Lazarus represent), we can be resurrected by the power of Spirit. No matter how sick we are mentally, emotionally, or physically, we can be healed. (B)

Resurrection is a restoration, a revitalization, a reclamation, a re-booting of our Christ potential every time we choose a Christed thought over a worldly thought. (B)

Reincarnations are resurrections. We get another chance to improve the last version of ourselves. (C)

Revelation 14:22

Metaphysically speaking, Revelation 14:22 means: "Blessed are those who purify their perspectives (wash their robes). By right of their enlightened consciousness (the narrow gate) they can become one with the Universal Life Force (Tree of Life) and live, move, and have their being in that exalted state of spiritual consciousness (enter the city)." (B)

Revelation 21:21b

In its literal interpretation Revelation 21:21b says: "The great street of the city was of pure gold, like transparent glass." Let's take a look at this verse from a metaphysical perspective: The 'great street' of the city is the Serpentine Energy, the Holy Spirit, the Kundalini Fire that flows up our spine when we are awakened. The 'city' is our Christ Consciousness. The 'gold' represents the enlightenment which comes from our elevated spiritual understanding. The 'transparent glass' symbolizes the knowledge that there is no separation between us and Spirit. (B)

Righteousness

Righteousness, metaphysically interpreted, means 'right thinking.' It means Christed thinking. It means keeping our thoughts at a spiritual octave. (B)

In the 23rd Psalm, the phrase "He leadeth me in the paths of righteousness for his name's sake" means that when we are connected with our Christ Self — when we have total awareness of our Oneness — our thoughts will be aligned with the highest, most elevated level of Spirit. We are free from error thinking! (C)

Ritual

We are fans of ritual and tradition as long as they provide traction for spiritual growth. (B)

Ritual is vitally important as a way for like-minded people to join together in a shared spiritual experience. Rituals bring a sense of community which allows us to connect at a heart level to the deeper Spiritual Truths which unite us. (C)

Romans 8:28

The Apostle Paul used the word *sunergeo* in Romans 8:28 to explain the dynamic synergy which occurs in human, divine, and cosmic cooperation. At its most basic interpretation, synergy means "unity, cooperation, working together." It carries with it the idea that the whole is greater than the sum of its parts. Cher and I believe this is what Romans 8:28 is telling us from a metaphysical perspective: When we synergize our human nature with our Christ Nature, we will be able to work all things together for good. (B)

Joining our individual spiritual gifts together is the only way we will ever experience the Divine Abundance and Peace we are meant to have. When we become possessive, power-driven, and self-focused, we sacrifice our Divine inheritance. Bil and I call this phenomenon Sync or Sink!

Sabbath

Sabbath — A call to cease from our personal efforts and rest in the consciousness of KNOWING. Experiencing a sabbath is to release any worry, any concerns or doubt — and stand firmly in Truth, knowing all is well. This is a celebration of completed activity! This is our time to "be still and know." We rejuvenate our spirit and refresh our soul. We take our 7th In-ing Stretch and know that it is good! (C)

Experiencing a Sabbath moment everyday so we can find our God connection is a radical prescription. It takes us out of the rat race. It takes our focus from the wasteland of hyperactivity to the peace and serenity of the 'still small voice.' (C)

> *Metaphysically, we experience the Sabbath every time we put worldly thoughts behind and focus on spiritual thoughts. A 2-minute prayer is a Sabbath. A 5-minute walk is a Sabbath. A 1-minute affirmation is a Sabbath. All of these are portable Sabbaths. (B)*

A Sabbath dissolves artificial urgencies. It helps us pace ourselves. It builds rest into our day. Hitting pause for a moment liberates us from the external hoopla. (B)

We encourage you to take a "Technology Sabbath" at least once a week. Unplug from everything electronic. Experience the joy of rediscovery as you allow your senses to revel in the bliss of contact with the real world. Notice the impact this has on your spirituality. (C)

Sacrifice

The true sacrifice of the Christ is not when a human being like Jesus of Nazareth is nailed to a cross. The sacrifice occurs when the Christ takes up residence as us in a limited, earth-bound human form at our birth. (B)

Salvation

We are saved each time we have a Christed thought, make a Christed choice, and take a Christed action. (C)

When the secular velocity of materialistic choices trumps spiritual discernment, soul growth is usually slowed and blunted. The effects of discordant thinking and acting create incongruencies in body, mind, and soul which increase the speed of our inevitable collision with our own shallowness. We must slow our secular velocity enough to speed up our spirituality. When we do that we are saved. (B)

True salvation should not be a product of fear or guilt. It occurs every moment we remain connected with the awareness of our Oneness. We are saved from the illusion of separation ... and *that* brings inner peace and joy. (C)

Philippians 2:12 says "Therefore, my dear friends, as you have always obeyed — not only in my presence, but now much more in my absence — continue to work out your salvation with fear and trembling..." This means that salvation is the process through which we personally transform our consciousness from a materialistic focus to a spiritual focus — thought by thought, intention by intention, choice by choice, action by action. When we do that we are saved. We are working out our own salvation! (B)

How much spiritual guidance do you give people verses letting them find out for themselves, particularily when it comes to enlightenment? The answer, as far as I'm concerned is: the path to our enlightenment doesn't mean we have to isolate ourselves from the guidance and experience of others who have traveled that path before us. Attaching ourselves to a guru, reading books written by 'enlightened' ones, attending higher consciousness seminars, attending Sunday services all contribute to our spiritual knowledge, but the master key to our enlightenment is we are responsible for our own enlightenment. (B)

Satan

Satan is not an anthropomorphic celestial being enticing us into a sinful life. Satan is the lower human nature in all of us, our shadow side. It is the self of us that can tempt us to do things we know are not for our highest good. Satan is the selfish, human, cunning, devious ego of limitation that motivates us to forsake our God-Self. (C)

Satan is not a being dressed in red, sporting a pitchfork and tail. Satan is not a being at all. Satan is the purely human tendency to consciously forsake the divinity within us through our error thoughts, intentions, choices, and actions. It is that aspect of us that purposefully chooses to give power to outer appearances instead of going to the Source of our good — our divine nature, the Christ as us. (B)

Science

Neuro-science has given us neuro-theology. I believe the two will marry, and along with quantum physics, will give us a trinity of higher thought that will shake the foundations of 'old time' religion. (B)

The good news is there is a strong feeling among a growing number of enlightened scientists and those in forward-thinking spiritual and religious communities that the subjects of cosmology, God, consciousness, and universal oneness on the one hand, and quantum physics and neurosciences on the other, are coming together to provide a unified description of the universe that just might see consciousness as the unified field. (B)

Even those of us who don't feel we are "up" on the latest scientific research can grasp the awareness that the gap between science and spirituality is closing. Science is catching up with what spirituality already knows. (C)

Second Coming

The Second Coming occurs when we realize we are divine beings in human form, and then, through disciplined practice, actualize our Christhood. When we do that, we will experience the Second Coming — the coming into direct conscious alignment with our Christ Self. It is the realization that we are the Christ expressing at the point of us. It is us, not the Christ, who comes — the Christ is already present as us. It is the result of many years, many human opportunities, to learn the Truth about who we really are. It is not an external cataclysmic event of the dreaded apocalypse predicted by literally-minded faith traditions. (B)

The Second Coming is not a point in time. It is a point in conscious awareness that we are Christed beings, have been Christed beings, and will be Christed beings. (B)

Self

When our "self" becomes consciously one with our "Self" we will have achieved the epitome of selfcare. (C)

The rider on a donkey theme in esoteric literature is a common metaphysical symbol. The rider represents our Higher Self, our Christ Self, an enlightened us, our Authentic Self, in metaphysical terms. The donkey is our lower self, the unquickened spiritual us, our human personality — characterized by stubbornness, material addictions, and an unwillingness to surrender to Spirit. (B)

Self-Knowledge

In order to unfold fully into our Christhood, our self-knowledge (human personality — little 's') must become Self-knowledge (Our Christ Self — capital 'S'). (B)

We must not cop out on our potential. Botched self-improvement is usually filled with error thoughts and actions that keep us from growing toward our potential. We must get to that place where we know that we know that we know we are spiritual beings having a human experience. (C)

I am always Bil-ing and re-Bil-ing. I am always compositing and re-compositing my human self, potting and repotting. My incarnational identity, my human-definition is always provisional. And that's good. Otherwise, I might go stale and remain static. Each consecutive moment of me is a nano version of me, an infinite me as well as a finite me, a me that is growing, expanding, deepening, becoming more and more like my Christ Self. (B)

Sense Consciousness

Sense consciousness is cosmetic consciousness. Its promiscuous affair with materialistic trappings is evidence of our ego's attachment to form. The sooner we prune ourselves from the worship of outer appearances the sooner we will awaken from our sleep. (B)

Sense consciousness is self-induced coma consciousness. The sooner we wake up the sooner we'll gain the clarity we need to be the best Christ we can be. (C)

Sermon on the Mount

The entire Sermon on the Mount series of talks could very well have been called Life's Little Instruction Papyrus Scroll. You can imagine the texting and tweeting that were going on. Cell phones were probably buzzing too. The hillside was alive with activity. Parents were shooing and shushing their children. People were asking people sitting next to them what Jesus said. People were interpreting what Jesus said to a nearby neighbor whose Aramaic was a second language. So, here's Jesus standing on top of the hill — all mic-ed up with his power point presentation, ready to deliver a powerful, dynamic keynote on a scorching summer day. (C)

One of my favorite sound bytes from Jesus' Sermon on the Mount, "Lay not up for yourselves treasures upon the earth," was hidden code for 'beware of materialistic thoughts and desires (treasures) that come from an egocentric consciousness (earth).' Moth and rust refer to corrosive, error thoughts and beliefs. Thieves are thoughts that deny our innate goodness and divinity. Instead he says, "lay up treasures in heaven," that is to say, cultivate a practice of adopting spiritually attuned thoughts and aspirations that come from a more elevated consciousness, a Christed consciousness (heaven). (B)

Serpent

One day we will discover our innate, fohatic, serpentine power and find ourselves winding ourselves around the core of our enlightenment. (B)

Service

Service is an unselfish, heart-felt attitude, not an event of convenience. (C)

We must blend our 'Martha-ed' service with our 'Mary-ed' interest in universal Truths. (B)

Service should not feel like a duty you have to perform. If you follow your interests, follow your joy, and follow your intuition, you will discover ways you can share your light with others ~ and you will receive far more than you ever give! (C)

Instead of 'servicing' error thoughts, we need to give them 'memorial services.' (B)

Sin

Sin is the "siGn" of our unenlightened humanness without God awareness in it which causes us to miss the mark in terms of embracing our innate divinity. Sin is the boogie woogie appeal of the senses. (B)

Our human nature doesn't cause our error thinking, choosing, and behaving — it is our lack of human nurture that contributes to our missing the mark. By nature we are the Christ in human clothing. (C)

When the Christ 'forgives' sin, it means our release from the heavy yoke of yesterday's sense-oriented consciousness and today's worldly intentions. It means at-one-ment with principle. The result of this heightened spiritual awareness is restoration and wholeness. (B)

Fear, anger, resentment, worry, greed, bearing false witness, and guilt have no nutritional value. (B)

Skin School

We are doing time here because the Only Begotten Son has become the Only Forgotten Son! We have forgotten we are the biological addresses of the Only Begotten Son. (B)

We tie ourselves up in human knots of frustration, anger, hurt, fear, and desire to retaliate. And this creates huge walls that bring the illusion of separation. This does not serve us, or others, in any positive way at all! And the key is this: even though it may appear that the source of our problem is that other person or situation, the TRUTH is, it is all happening within us! We may not have any control over others, but we have one hundred percent control over our response ... and that makes all the difference! (C)

According to ancient wisdom, when we became fixated on our ability to create and accumulate things at the expense of our spiritual connection, we fell from grace. We rationalized ourselves and coveted ourselves into lack and limitation. (B)

Son of Man

In the New Testament, Jesus said: "As Moses lifted up the staff in the wilderness, so must the Son of Man be lifted up...." Jesus made an incredible claim. First, He was equating His power with the serpentine power of the legendary healing staff. Secondly, He was saying that the intertwining of that vital life force was the very essence of who He was. I believe the Son of Man that Jesus referred to is the human personality which must be lifted up to its Christ nature. The wilderness where Moses found himself is our sense consciousness. The staff is our spinal cord. Moses himself represents our ability to lift ourselves out of negativity and sense attachments. (B)

Song of Solomon (Song of Songs) 2:15

In the Song of Solomon, 2:15, NIV version, it says: *"Catch for us the foxes, the little foxes that ruin the vineyards, our vineyards that are in bloom."* Metaphysically, the "foxes" are negative thoughts that can destroy our attitude, our perspective, and our experiences. 'Vineyard' symbolizes the realm of Divine Substance that is there, in potential, for us! One little fox, negative thought, doesn't seem too bad; but if you feed him, others will join him, and pretty soon, they have taken over your consciousness! (C)

Speaking in Tongues

Speaking in tongues symbolizes our ability to communicate deeper meanings of hidden Truths. It means we can communicate esoteric Truths, metaphorical Truths, mystical Truths, cabalistic Truths, theosophical Truths, and metaphysical Truths in such a way that people can understand them. (B)

We believe people are ready to hear a metaphysical message. They are hungry for it — but they are coming from many different faith traditions and perspectives. So, before we present metaphysical material we take a moment to make the connection with our Christ Nature. That way we will be guided to speak in tongues (share our Truth in a way that will make sense for our audiences). Then we trust the process — trust our connections to our highest and best Self to know exactly what to say and how to say it. (C)

Spirit

We cannot *not* be connected to Spirit! Why? Because we are Spirit expressing as us. We are the beneficiaries of a divine coupling at birth. (C)

We are filigreed Spirit in human form. (B)

We must offer Spirit the cradle It deserves. (B)

Anytime we fall, anywhere we fall, anyway we fall, we fall into Spirit. (C)

Spiritual Apps

Become a Spiritual Techie! Bil and I have looked at the techie phrase, "There's an App for That!" We've explored Spiritual Apps, Tweets, and Texts! Are you ready for the "411" on Spiritual Techno-Slang? If you've spent any time at all with email or texting, you're familiar with all the shortcut slang that is used. Techno-slang has reached an all-time high. We believe it would be extremely useful to create a special Spiritual Techno-Slang — designed to help us quickly and painlessly remind ourselves and others of the Truth of who we are, and the spiritual principles on which we stand. For example, here are five Spiritual Techno-Slang acronyms you can start using immediately: LTYI (Listen To Your Intuition); TY4S (Thank You For Sharing); BSAK (Be Still And Know); ICYD (I See Your Divinity); IMGX (I Am God Expressing). (C)

Why not create Spiritual Tweets that capture the essence of your Truth walk, and what you want to see manifested in your life? We can "Spiritually Tweet" the Truth of who we are—God expressing at the point of us! With that clarity of focus, we are ready to advance (never "retweet") to the most elevated levels of our spiritual consciousness! (C)

Texting has become a worldwide obsession and it is a great metaphor for our spiritual practice! So what is the equivalent to texting, from a Spiritual perspective? It would be a quick, easy, readily available and always responded to form of communication that keeps us connected with Spirit. Bil and I call prayer, affirmations, and denials spiritual texts. (C)

If Jesus were right here, right now, He might say: "No matter what situations we find ourselves in, no matter what emotions we are experiencing, no matter what challenges our life's journey presents to us, from a spiritual perspective, there's an app for that!" (C)

Spiritual Cataracts

A fishbowl mentality is for those who choose to live limited lives. They are for those who settle for self-imposed enclosures, fences, and walls. People can choose to remain in a fishbowl of anger, in a fishbowl of unforgiveness, in the fishbowl of hatred. They can stay in an ocean of self-doubt, and fear, and worry. But the view from these fishbowls is distorted. Fishbowls, like limited perspectives, are for people who want to live in the past. They're for people who are afraid to give up old perspectives and worn out beliefs. Who are fixated on old assumptions. Who wear misinformation like badges of honor. Who still believe in an anthropomorphic God. The result is spiritual cataracts. (B)

Choosing to think prosperously, speak prosperously, and act prosperously does NOT mean you go around with rose colored glasses, in total denial of what may be happening in your world! It means acknowledging the facts of your current situation, then planting your feet firmly on the ground of Truth to deal with it from a consciousness of Truth Principles. Otherwise, you're subject to spiritual cataracts. (C)

Spiritual Echo-nomics

Spiritual ECHO-nomics is a phrase Bil and I use to describe this Truth: what we send out comes back to us multiplied! So we invite people to create echoes in their lives that are positive, prosperous, and congruent with the spiritual principles they profess. (C)

Spiritual Economics

The economies of scale in spiritual growth are prayer, meditation, metaphysical education, service, faith, love and discernment. (B)

Spiritual economics is the economy of thoughts, the economy of words, and the economy of actions! As we become more aware of our innate divinity, and practice living from that Truth, we discover the incredible importance of spiritual economics. (C)

Spiritual economics is prosperity shaping. You have the right — no, the responsibility — no, the *privilege* of putting your stamp of God-Consciousness on everything you see, feel, hear, taste, smell, and intuit. (B)

Wall Street doesn't determine our prosperity because Wall Street is not our

Source. A government stimulus package will never be our savior because it is not our Source. Downturns in the economy can't handcuff us because they're not, never have been, and never will be what determine or limit our good. (B)

Spiritual Growth

Spiritual growth occurs when we "Shoot from the Lip!" SHOOT is an acronym, standing for: Spiritually Honoring Only One Truth! Every affirmation we create must be grounded in the Truth of No Separation. (C)

You don't have to go to India, or Tibet, or recluse yourself on a mountaintop, or sit at the feet of a guru in an Ashram somewhere. All you need to do is go within, where the Kingdom of God is. (C)

Personal, professional, and spiritual transformation are hard work — but only to a point. Eventually, through disciplined effort and commitment, you become the change you want to see. You become less tempted by old habits, beliefs, and assumptions. (B)

A turtle's shell grows at the same rate as the rest of the turtle, so there is hardly a need of concern of the turtle getting too fat for its shell. When the shell begins to look as if it is coming apart, it is merely growing; discarding portions of the old with incoming segments of new. As we grow spiritually, we, too, need to discard the things that are no longer working for us at our new spiritual level! Perform regular mental check-ups to be sure your thoughts are congruent with the Truth principles you live by! Anything out of alignment needs to go! (C)

I encourage you to move beyond the erroneous belief that you are here just to learn lessons. You have lessons all right, and sometimes they are harsh lessons, but your lessons are the consequences of your error thoughts and actions. They are effects, not causes. You are here to become one with and fulfill your Christ Nature — just like Jesus did when He became one with His Christ Nature. (B)

Bil and I love to ballroom dance. One thing you learn as you progress in your dance lessons is that every single part of a choreography is made up of dance elements, and once you learn a number of elements you can create dance patterns made up of elements. Once you know a number of dance patterns, it makes it very easy to learn a new routine quickly. Our spiritual growth occurs pretty much the same way. Once we integrate the elements of prayer, meditation, study, outreach, and attending services into regular patterns of daily practice, we will notice substantial spiritual growth. (C)

Each of our thoughts, words, and actions is a soul sequel. Unlike most movie sequels which are generally embarrassing attempts at movie-making, our soul sequels must continue to improve or remain re-makes of our error consciousness. (B)

Too often we wait for things to come to us. People who grow the most are the ones who take the initiative to expand their spiritual horizons. They are always questioning, challenging, experiencing, putting themselves in situations where they hear new ideas and beliefs. So, read a few paragraphs from a spiritually-challenging book, or attend a higher consciousness class, or meet someone for coffee to discuss spiritual insights. Keep a journal with your aha's. Every day, find a way to take a look at a new way of applying the Truth principles you know. (C)

In her book, The Artists' Way, Julia Cameron says, "I build the necklace of my day, stringing together choices that form artful living." I would re-word that to say, "I build the necklace of my day, stringing together spiritual tweets that empower me to master the art of living." (C)

According to neurologists it takes less than two weeks for neurons to form new axons and dendrites. What this is telling us is significant influences in our lives, like witnessing a breath-taking sunset, dealing with the emotions of a highly competitive sports event, being involved with a close call in an accident, receiving a diagnosis of a life-threatening health challenge, or listening to a riveting Sunday Truth talk, can trigger a rapid rewiring of our brain's circuitry. Knowing this, Cher and I take our Sunday Truth talks very seriously. We want to be catalysts of transformational neural rewiring, rewiring that helps people move toward being the best Christs they can be. (B)

Spiritual Hydration

When we become spiritually dehydrated (disconnected from the flow of living water that is our awareness of our Oneness), we make poor choices and decisions. Each poor choice takes us deeper into the spiral of fear, negativity, and depression. The best way out is to avoid it in the first place, by practicing good spiritual hydration! That means having a regular habit of consuming spiritual thoughts, meditating, connecting with our center of Oneness — so we are always filled with the living water — the Indwelling Christ Presence. (C)

Spirituality

People confuse spirituality with being perpetually solemn. There are times in our spiritual practice when we are quiet and still as we pray, meditate, and listen for inner guidance. But there are also times for joy! Biblical references, depending on the translation, list over 350 references for praise, over 240 for joy, over 150 for rejoicing, over 180 for singing; and 40 refer to dance! (C)

Be a spiritual lighthouse instead of a religious flashlight. (B)

Spiritual Obstetrics

Become a new you-ologist where you are potted and repotted each day, born and reborn each day. We call this spiritually oriented 'new you process' spiritual obstetrics. (B)

Spiritual Orthopedics

Walking the spiritual path on practical feet requires spiritual orthopedics if we want to step confidently and lively toward our Christhood. It doesn't matter if our steps are on bare feet or shoed feet, big feet or small feet, white feet or brown feet or red feet or yellow feet, tired feet or energetic feet. Each step is a tithe toward our becoming one with our Christ Nature. The spiritual orthopedics of any Truth walk requires steadfast faith, supported by love, wisdom, and zeal, multiplied by understanding and strength, and a penchant for divinely ordering every experience we have from a consciousness of our oneness with Spirit. (B)

Spiritual Practice

We grow into our Christ Essence every time we "practice the Presence." (B)

It is not enough to know God is absolute good everywhere present. The real question is, do you live that Truth? If you allow fear or anger to take power within you, then you aren't living the Truth you know. Denying that power, and affirming that God is absolute good and all is well is living the Truth. (C)

No one can grow your spirituality for you. No one, not even the person who loves you the most, can make you a more spiritual person. (B)

Stop talking about what you believe and put your spiritual practice into action — every day, in everything you think, choose, and do! It's time for less bark and more wag, so you can master the art of living by walking the spiritual path on practical feet! (C)

We've got to 'man-up' and 'woman-up' when it comes to our spiritual growth. (B)

The most noticeable kind of spiritual growth is heart-to-head resuscitation. (B)

When we identify error thinking and, through denials, refute its power, error thoughts depart, leaving a void which must be filled. If it is not filled, the error thinking will return, and become even stronger than it was initially, making us more skeptical and frustrated with the world of appearance than when we began our spiritual journey. This is why it is so important to create a regular practice of prayer and meditation, coupled with denials and affirmations, to refuel and rejuvenate ourselves as we continue strengthening our lives built on spiritual principles. (C)

Use prayer, meditation, and affirmations as spiritual guardrails. (B)

A life built on prayer apps, meditation apps, affirmation apps, and denial apps is a life built on solid spiritual ground. (C)

Woodpeckers are built for shock. They're hardheaded. Just like our friends the woodpeckers, we have built-in shock absorbers: Truth principles are shock absorbers. Our openness to deeper Truths and higher spiritual principles is a shock absorber. Prayer and meditation are premium shock absorbers. Forgiveness is an unfailing shock deflector. Our willingness to sidestep slights and gossip is a shock absorber. Accepting a heartfelt hug is a wonderful shock absorber. Truth principles are unfailing shock absorbers. (B)

Become CONSCIOUS of your CONSCIOUSNESS! Wherever you are, just ask yourself, "Am I coming from my most elevated level of Consciousness in this moment? Am I acting out of the Truth Principles I believe?" If not, ask, "How is this lower level of awareness serving me? (C)

Spiritual Purpose

There is no one else in the world who can do what you do, the way you do it! You are a beautiful and unique spiritual being, with many gifts to share. Recognize that you make an impact on every life you touch. So let your light shine as you walk the spiritual path on practical feet. (C)

Your purpose, my purpose, humankind's purpose is to recognize, develop, fulfill, and actualize our innate divinity. (B)

Spiritual Teachers

All of the world's great spiritual teachers have one thing in common. It doesn't matter who they are, where they're from, or in what era they live. It includes the gurus and spiritual masters who preceded Jesus, the Buddha, Krishna, Lao Tzu — and those who will come after. In every case, the one distinct thing they have in common is — they spent their entire ministry in the same place. Sounds incredible doesn't it? But it's true. Jesus, Krishnamurti, the Dalai Lama, Mother Teresa, Thich Nhat Hanh have all spent their ministries in the same place. They have devoted all of their time and energy there. As do all great spiritual teachers. That place is a place Cher and I call the 'Subconscious Depot.' It's our subconsciousness — the place where all of our human experiences, patterns of behavior, life scripts, faulty coping patterns, and egocentric defense mechanisms are warehoused. And it's a place spiritual teachers have been trying to get humankind out of for centuries. (B)

Still Small Voice

Sometimes the decibel level of the "Still Small Voice" is deafening. When the volume is turned up, the calling becomes loud and clear — not in an audible sense, but in an inner knowingness which is unmistakably clear. (B)

Switch your allegiance from 'guru' worship to listening to the 'still small voice' within. (B)

Guidance comes from deep within. Some call it Intuition; others call it the Still Small Voice; others call it God. No matter what label you give It, the only way to take advantage of this Divine Wisdom is to "be still and know." (C)

Struggle

When you are faced with millstones like fear, worry, and guilt, use them as milestones toward your spiritual transformation and joy! (C)

We all struggle from time to time. However, the warning label on a can of Drano gives us a clue on how we can clear up the blockages in our lives. The warning on a can of Drano is actually pretty clear and specific, and makes a lot of sense! What if there was a warning label on such a thing as Spiritual Drano? It might go something like this: Spiritual Drano is extremely powerful, and is not to be taken lightly! Never mix it with fear, illusion, or belief in separation! Do not combine with worry, anger, frustration, envy, negative thinking, or doubt. Stay in touch with your Higher Power in the event clogs appear to be too extreme for your human consciousness to handle. And above all, make the use of Spiritual Drano a part of your daily routine, to avoid any recurrences of old clogs or the appearance of new ones! (C)

Suffering

Suffering is human spiritual unfoldment calibrated to its lowest possible setting. Most of us are filled with warehouses of repressed emotions which become lactic limitations that slow our spiritual growth. (B)

Why do we suffer? Here's my answer. Are you ready? We suffer because we believe we are separate from God. And because we believe we are separate from God, we believe we are separate from one another. And because we deny our oneness with one another, we build and perpetuate a collective error consciousness which gives power to outer appearances that reinforce our belief in our separateness from God. That sequence of warped Mind Action is the cause of all suffering. (B)

Despite the limitations we experience as spiritual beings in human form, Bil and I believe — absolutely believe, positively believe — that all of the sicknesses and illnesses we face in this life are not only unnecessary but were never part of the original plan for our lives. (C)

Remember the quote, "Don't sweat the small stuff — and it's all small stuff!" Well, I beg to differ. Some things are small stuff: like computer problems, traffic lights, and irritating people. But some of it IS big stuff: like the loss of a job, a life-threatening diagnosis, the unexpected death of a loved one, or a heart-wrenching emotional relationship issue. These are big 'stuffs.' And we need a way to work our way through them. We need more than platitudes to deal with them. This is when prayer and meditation can help us bring meaning, grace, and peace to any situation. (C)

Jesus did not say in John 10:10 — "I came that you might have suffering and have it more abundantly." He said — "I came that you might have LIFE and have it more abundantly." So, pre-prayer yourself to live life more abundantly. (B)

Superman Christ

Negative thinking, selfish aggrandizement, racial and gender prejudice, hurtful actions, and religious intolerance are all Kryptonite to the Superman Christ potential in all of us. (B)

We have a superhero within us. It is the Superman Christ. The Christ within us is that super-hero! The day we identify with our Superman Christ/Superwoman Christ and not with fictitious superheroes 'out there' will be the day we master our human experience. (B)

Thanksliving

Cultivating a consistent consciousness of thanksgiving by becoming aware of the myriad opportunities to express our gratitude and praise is the essence of thanksliving. (C)

I Thessalonians 5:16 says: "Rejoice. In everything give thanks." And in Chapter 1, verse 2 it says, "Give thanks to God always." Notice it says be thankful in all things and not for all things. We do not have to be grateful for disease, or disharmony, or cancer, or a heart attack, or a harsh lesson. The scripture passage encourages us to be grateful in the midst of our human challenges. Be grateful for what? Why, be grateful for our ability to work all things that happen to us for good. (B)

Third Coming

The Third Coming will occur when people all over the world actualize their divinity and witness the fulfillment of the divinity in others. We will experience the Third Coming when the entire world is Christ-filled, Buddha-filled, Great Spirit-filled. (B)

Thought Power

It isn't enough to know that everything in the manifest realm has its beginning in thought. Are you using that power to manifest the reality YOU desire and deserve? (C)

We will see more clearly when we Feng Shui our thinking. (B)

Thoughts have 'echo power.' They always return the call sent out. Like an echo, the response is always the consciousness from which the call springs. The louder the call, that is, the more pronounced the Truth or limitation, the greater the response — thoughts held in mind produce after their kind. (C)

Just because an old thought pattern or perspective comes into our awareness doesn't mean we have lost spiritual ground. 'Error thoughts' are simply residues of our past. They'll pop up now and again. They're the ego's way of holding on to its eroding authority. (C)

Bickering thoughts are generally symptomatic of a thought rolodex full of error thoughts. The best thing we can do is to delete error thoughts from our consciousness so we can move past the mental bedlam that blocks our good. (B)

What do you have in your thought bank that needs to be weeded out? What old ideas, beliefs, and habits are inconsistent with the Truth principles you have learned? (C)

Suppose you're sitting on your front porch. A convertible comes by and someone shouts, "Get in!" And so you get in. You don't know where it's going but you get in anyway. Later that same day you're sitting on the porch again and an SUV comes by. Someone says, "Get in." You get in although you're not sure where it's going or how long it's going to take. Later that evening you're sitting on that same porch and a truck comes by. Someone shouts, "Get in …" and so … (you get the picture). Suppose each of those vehicles represents an error thought. Just because a false assumption surfaces in our consciousness doesn't mean we have to go with it. We don't have to let outdated beliefs or cosmetic assumptions take us for a ride. (B)

Tithing

Tithing is really an acronym. It stands for: 'The Indwelling Truth Harmoniously Increases Never-ending Good.' (C)

Unless your tithing is from a giving consciousness, all of the one-comma or two-comma tithing you do will not bring the financial, emotional, or spiritual return you seek. (B)

Switch your perspective from a philosophy of getting to a spirituality of giving. (B)

Tithing is a word with a lot of baggage attached to it, and I want to reframe it! People get into such a huff about issues surrounding tithing, like do I tithe from "net or gross?" or "what percent?" or "does it all go my church, or do charitable contributions count?" All these questions come from the attitude of tithing as a LAW — something we are forced to do, something we have to do. And from that consciousness, tithing becomes a burden. Let's ditch the baggage, and tithe from a Consciousness of Giving! (C)

Transcendence

John Gribbon uses a book analogy to explain the Multiverse: "The universes that make up the Multiverse are like the pages in an infinitely thick book, with each page representing a universe which is tantalizingly close to the universe next to it." Jesus, it seems, walked from one page into another, from one dimension into another, from one universe into another. At his level of consciousness he wasn't limited by space, or time, or physical form, or religious denominational bias. (B)

Transformation

We transform ourselves every time we have a Christed thought. The effect these divinely-charged thoughts have on us spiritually, emotionally, and cellularly is truly transformative. Neuroscientists are very aware of the rewiring and restructuring effects our thoughts have on our physiology and biology. (B)

Tree of Knowledge of Good and Evil

The Tree of Knowledge is the space-time based consciousness of quantum beings such as ourselves, who have chosen the duality and separation schools of learning as our reconnection tools with Spirit. Sacred tree symbolism is found in Jewish, Shamanic, Hindu, Buddhist, Assyrian, Egyptian, Sumerian, Toltec, Norse and Christian faith traditions. (B)

Tree of Life

The Tree of Life is the eternal, foliated, universal God Consciousness which underwrites all beingness and nonbeingness. Its 'roots' are said to be firmly placed in the firmament of the Eternal Isness and Its 'canopy' extending into the realm of physicality. (B)

Trinity

The Holy Trinity's outpicturing is the involuting of Godness evoluting as us. (B)

Most people are fascinated with the intrigue and mystery of a love triangle. You may be one of them. Love triangles, it seems, are the opium of Hollywood and the amphetamines of the masses. They've been part of the human condition ever since there's been a human condition. However, the 'love triangle' Cher and I recommend is a spiritual one — the Holy trinity: Father, Son, and Holy Ghost. The key to understanding the Trinity is to see It as the Eternal Cosmic Creative Process which produces all that is manifest from the unmanifest. That whole cosmic process is the Ultimate Love Triangle because the Infinite becomes Intimate as us. (B)

One thing really struck Bil and I as we had the incredible opportunity of visiting the Mayan ruins of Tulum and Chitzen Itza. As we admired the amazing pyramids and listened to the guides share the mind-boggling feats of these people, in terms of their astrological powers, their mathematical genius, and their architectural prowess, the fact remained that we were looking at ruins! And this reminded us of how often people focus on the external, building monuments of stone, steel, marble, and glass in an attempt to discover their divinity — when all along we really need to go within, knowing we have that eternal spark of the pyramid power of the Trinity which can never fall into ruins. (C)

Truth

A Truth walk is the path of least resistance to unfolding into our Christ Nature. (C)

Our Truth walk is the path of God-ness indivisiblized as us. It is our conscious entrainment toward our Christ Nature. (B)

Be willing to release what you thought was truth to make room for greater Truth. (C)

"You shall know the Truth, and the Truth shall make you free!" These are the words of Jesus — and what great news. From a metaphysical perspective this passage means that eventually, we will discover that we are Christ [the Truth] expressing as us and that we can transcend any and all human limitations [be set free]. (C)

We are the Truth becoming truthized. (B)

All of the truths we know are merely approximations of Truth. No particular faith tradition has a patent on truth, including the faith tradition Cher and I have chosen for our spiritual growth. (B)

The Hebrew word for 'truth' is *emet*. If you drop the first letter you have the Hebrew word *met*, which means 'death.' What has to 'die' is our irresponsible belief in separation and duality. Otherwise, we will remain stuck in sense consciousness and continue to be blinded by its egocentric attachment to the world of outer appearances. (B)

Truth Principles

We know the principles ... we speak the principles ... but what happens when we hit rough spots, when life throws us a curve, when we find ourselves in a dark night of the soul experience? Do we stand UP for our Truth principles? It's easy to believe in Truth principles when everything is going great. But when things go wrong (disappointments, illness, stress, fear, relationship issues, money problems) we neglect to apply the Truth principles we know when they could be the most beneficial. When life throws us a curve, we need to Amp UP our time at Headquarters, the Kingdom of God within us. We need to make sure we are prayed UP every day, keep UP our faith, wise UP, and speak UP using denials and affirmations. These are all investments in Upping our Consciousness! If that's being Uppity, give me uppity! (C)

Don't follow Truth principles to prove they're true. Follow Truth principles to prove yourself true to Truth principles. (B)

Unforgivable Sin

From a human point of view there are many irreconcilable differences. From a spiritual perspective there's only one. It's so important we want you to know about it because it's an unforgivable irreconcilable 'sin.' This unforgivable irreconcilable sin is not about working on the Sabbath. Nor is it coveting your neighbor's stock portfolio. It's not about lying, or bearing false witness, or stealing. Nor is it about cheating on your income taxes. It's not even secretly replacing the golf ball you couldn't find with another one and not adding strokes to your score. The irreconcilable sin that is alluded to in the Bible is called the unforgivable sin. What is the unforgivable sin? Read Matthew 12:31-32 in your favorite Bible interpretation. There are two important words we need to remember: unforgiveable and blasphemy. They are central for understanding what this passage means. Unforgiveness means failing to give up the false for the true. If we repeat error time and time again and continue repeating it, we're likely to, well, keep repeating it. It's the repetition that makes it unforgiveable. Blasphemy is the second important word in the Matthew account. Blasphemy is a powder keg word. As it is used here it refers to blasphemy against the Holy Spirit. And blasphemy against the Holy Spirit is denying our divinity. If we blaspheme, deny our divinity, we won't be able to reconcile the difference between Truth and error, between our spiritual self and our material self, between being enlightened and being clueless. (B)

When we remember that "forgiveness" means giving up the false for the true, and "sin" means missing the mark, then the only "unforgiveable sin" is when we hold on to the false and continue missing the mark! (C)

Unity

Unity comes when we are able to honor diversity while still beholding the Divinity within each and every person. (C)

If I can unite within myself harmonious thoughts and attitudes about all of the faith traditions (Christians, Muslims, Hindus, Buddhists, Native American, Catholics, and so on) as well as their esoteric elements, I can prepare in myself a localized reunion of a divided humanity. Bringing together what is divided is a process that begins in my heart and then is expressed from my own Christ center. We — I'm speaking for all of us — cannot force unity. If we do, all we get is a political union, one that is doomed to division and separatism. If we want true spiritual unity, we must transcend all forms and patterns of division in our own hearts and minds first. (B)

Unity "out there" will come when there's unity within us. The longer it takes us to unify our consciousness, the longer it will take for unity to unfold between people, countries, and continents. (C)

What if we paraphrased the Preamble to the Constitution to describe humankind's spiritual progress? It would go something like this: We the people of Planet Earth, in order to form a more perfect union; establish a system of positive, practical, progressive spirituality; insure domestic tranquility; provide healing opportunities and metaphysical teachings for ourselves and our posterity; do ordain and establish this spiritual philosophy for our mutual spiritual growth and the spiritual growth of the generations that follow. (B)

Universality

Universality is multiple multiplicity in harmonious cosmic complicity. (B)

Universal Substance

Many think of supply as receiving. Supply is not income; it is outgo — it is invisible Universal Substance. Let's say that again: Many think of supply as receiving. Supply is not income; it is outgo — it is invisible Universal Substance ... (Do we need to say it again? Have you got it?) You create a flow of substance through a consciousness of giving; you create a consciousness of giving by giving. Start the flow of giving, and you will start the flow of supply. Giving is acknowledging that Universal Substance is everpresent, and you are standing in the midst of it. (C)

When we do not have faith in the availability of Universal Substance we tend to cling, to consume, to hold onto, to covet. Our good, in potential, is a thought, an intention, a choice away — if we free ourselves from blockages, from attachments, from old habits. (B)

The omnipresent spiritual substance from which comes all visible wealth is never depleted. It is with us all the time and responds to our faith in it and our demands on it. **It** is not affected by talk of hard times, though **we** are affected, because our thoughts and words govern our demonstrations. The unfailing resource is always ready to give. (C)

Supply is not something that comes to us. It comes through us. Supply is not something that comes to us. It comes through us. Supply is not something that comes to us. It comes through us. It is an inside-out process. (B)

Universe

By its very nature the universe is expanding. It is filled with thought forms like supernovas, singularities, quasars, galaxies, parallel universes, cosmic inflation, black holes, binary star systems, and rare quantum beings like us. This expansion mirrors our own expansion in consciousness. (B)

Up until now it was believed that our universe was the only universe and that it was created by the Big Bang. Most physicists today agree that there were a number of little Big Bangs — one of which was ours. Cosmologists have recently proposed that our universe is part of a Multiverse which has always existed. A Multiverse, they speculate, is a unified field which contains many universes. This unified field, also known as the zero point field, is the quantum extension of our evolving consciousness. (B)

The universe is the purposeful inhalation and exhalation of Universal Substance breathing life into a cosmic idea. (B)

In Genesis 1:31 we read that on the sixth day of creation, 'God saw all that had been created and behold it was very good.' That's actually one of two mistranslations in the Genesis account. In the original Aramaic the verse does not read 'behold it was very good,' but 'behold it was a unified order.' Sounds quantum, doesn't it? And the other mistranslation is the second word in Genesis 1:1. It says, "In the beginning..." The 'the' is the mistranslation. In the original Aramaic it says, "In a beginning..." which squares with the 'unified order' theme, and also with the Multiverse theory in quantum physics. (B)

Our bodies literally hold the entire history of the universe in our cells, atoms, and molecules. The helium and hydrogen atoms in us are the Adam and Eve atoms, the parent atoms of all other atoms which came out of our little Big Bang. The iron atoms in our blood carrying oxygen to our cells came from exploding white dwarf stars. The oxygen we breathe came from exploding supernovas. Most of the carbon in the carbon dioxide we exhale came from planetary nebulas. We are truly made of star stuff. (B)

We are bundles of potential, expansion, and growth. Our whole being is wired for expansion and growth. We are born as sparks of Spirit with an inborn urge to return as quickly as we can to our true nature. (B)

We have created this playground called the universe to discover the physical dimensions of beingness. But in doing so we lost our conscious connection with our eternal beingness. We forgot who we really are and what we can achieve as flesh and blood expressions of Spirit. We have become attached to the pleasures of physical sensation and forgotten that material things are simply outer expressions of an inner spiritual realm that is endless, unlimited, and eternal. (B)

Unquiet City

All of the violence, conflict, cynicism and desperation we find today occur in the unquiet city. The unquiet city is human consciousness. It is a consciousness of separation perpetuated by well-meaning religious organizations and governmental institutions who, by their very natures, produce violent, conflicting, cynical and desperate "thought communities" within the human personality. These "communities" or "cities" are belief systems that keep us off balance emotionally and spiritually. The unquiet city is a consciousness without the awareness of its oneness with Spirit. (B)

Violence

Violence feeds on itself. It is cannibalistic and contagious. Erasing 'criminal mimes' once and for all must come from a consciousness of unconditional love, resolute forgiveness, unfailing compassion, and courageous education. Capital punishment is not the answer, and neither is building more prisons. The only way to silence violence is to love it out of existence in human consciousness. (B)

When we witness a violent act on television, we can send our energy of love out to everyone involved ... even (and perhaps most especially) to the perpetrator of the violence. Hidden deep within is the Divinity that must come forth before peace can prevail. (C)

Virgin Birth

Metaphysically speaking, a virgin birth occurs every time a new truth dawns on us while we are in a high spiritual state of consciousness. The virginity represents the undefiled and purified stillness of mind in us that gives birth to (becomes consciously aware of) the Christ Pattern within us. (B)

Vow

Vows are heart resolutions, not lip gloss. (C)

See vows as allies in your spiritual growth. They are vocal witnesses confirming that the outer you is becoming aligned with the spiritual you. They are registering your intention to become consciously one with your innate divinity. (B)

"Wait" Lifting

There are those who are quite satisfied with only a literal interpretation of scripture, or see no need to explore hidden spiritual Truths, or simply fail to apply spiritual Truths at all. When all three of these conditions exist they represent a sterile state of mind — a barren fig tree. Knowing Truth and then not applying it turns out to be a barren experience. (B)

Walking the Talk

When a child thrusts his or her small hand into yours, it may be smeared with ice cream or jelly, or there may be a wart under the right thumb, or a colorful Band-Aid on a little finger. But the most important thing about this little hand is that it is a hand that is the preamble of a future adult. This hand someday may hold a Bible or a copy of the Daily Word. It may play a church piano, or gently dress a wound, or pull someone to safety. Or it could hold a revolver, or tremble wretchedly as it grasps a drug needle, or it could set the timer on a bomb. People who do these things were once innocent, impressionable, teachable children. (B)

Each of us is a walking commercial for Truth. Are you worthy of the endorsement? Do people know Truth by the way they see you in action? Our words mean nothing unless our actions epitomize them. (C)

Walking on Water

Metaphysically speaking we 'walk on water' every time we rise above the negative emotions associated with our human experience. (B)

I love the 'walking on water' story in Matthew, Chapter 14, because there is such richness in the metaphysical interpretation! Even when we are surrounded by unsettled emotions, fear, worry (represented by the stormy waves of the lake), inner peace and oneness is right there (Jesus was walking on the water, above the raging emotions.) But there are those outside voices crying in fear, refusing to recognize that Divine Presence. When we trust, we are able to step out in faith and rise above the storms of emotion. But when our "head voice" starts talking ("What makes you think you can do this? What are you thinking?"), we take our attention away from that connection with Spirit, and we begin to sink into the negative emotions of the world. But the moment we reclaim our oneness (Lord, save me!), we realize we have never lost that oneness! It is there in that instant! And we wonder how we could have ever doubted! (C)

War

All wars are an unhealthy and frightened ego's attempt to force Spirit's hand. Much like Judas sought to force Jesus to use His considerable spiritual powers to rule the world, the ambitious Judas of us (our aggrandizing ego) seeks to tempt the Christ of us to use its Omnipotence for worldly gain. (B)

The external wars in our world are reflections of the internal wars going on within our consciousness. Until we find peace within, we will never experience peace in our outer world. (C)

Wealth

Too often we equate wealth with money. True wealth comes when we are able to realize it doesn't matter how much money we amass until we have inner peace and harmony; once we have inner peace and harmony, it doesn't matter how much money we amass. (C)

We are rich in direct proportion to what we can do without. Our lives can be enormously richer when we do without certain things, certain relationships, certain foods, certain habits, certain beliefs, certain assumptions, certain choices. (B)

White Light

Consciousness researcher William Braud's studies on 'psychological shielding' revealed that we could mentally block or prevent any outside influences we didn't want. I thought of the 'white light' technique Cher and I have been using for 20 years. Some of you may use the White Light technique. It's the one where you mentally surround yourself with a cocoon of white light to protect yourself from harm, from things like someone else's cold, or cough, or illness, or injury. Braud's studies confirm our belief that consciousness is the ground of all being. (B)

Transform negative situations by sending beams of white light out from your heart center to surround everyone and every thing involved. You will be amazed at the impact this has, not only on the situation, but on how you are able to respond to it. (C)

Make White Light your Spiritual headlight. (C)

Wholeness

All of us are on the road to Emmaus. Metaphysically, Emmaus means wholeness and reclamation. When we reach that level of wholeness, that level of heightened spiritual awareness, we will reclaim our divine inheritance. (B)

Widowhood

Metaphysically, widowhood represents half of something. When we study Truth principles, but doubt they'll work for us, we become widows and widowers. Widowhood is love without commitment, intellect without intuition, head without heart, ambition without wisdom, knowledge without faith, literal Bible translation without metaphysical interpretation. (B)

Winged Globe

An idea divinely ordered, a human personality transitioning toward its Christedness, a soul being lifted by Spirit, humankind experiencing the Third Coming, bitterness morphing into forgiveness, coma consciousness being raised to Christ Consciousness, selfishness amped-up to generosity are all leaps in consciousness symbolized by the winged globe. (B)

Wisdom

Wisdom is logic in a hurry. (B)

Chapter 9 in the Book of Proverbs discusses and contrasts two opposite houses. It says that every one of us has to choose which house we'll live in. Metaphysically each house represents a state of consciousness. One house (state of consciousness) is the house of wisdom; the other house (state of consciousness) is the house of foolishness. A fool is someone who is deficient in judgment, someone who doesn't use good sense, someone who shows a lack understanding. [The Hebrew word for wise is very interesting. It means "skillful...practical at living life."] Proverbs 9:1 says, "Wisdom has built her house, she has hewn out her seven pillars ..." It's interesting that the verse mentions seven pillars. Pillars are basically supports which hold the building in place, giving it its strength. In the Bible the number "7" symbolizes completeness or perfection. The point is that when we choose to come from the consciousnes of wisdom, we quicken the seven energetic power centers called chakras (the seven pillars). This strengthens the foundation on which we live our lives, so we can more fully manifest the Truth of who we are. (C)

When the whine is in, wisdom is out. (B)

You have within you the wisdom symbolized by Solomon, the wisdom to know what to release and what to affirm ... the wisdom to make choices from your highest consciousness, recognizing there is no separation, only oneness. (C)

Divine Wisdom IS the Breakfast of Champions! (C)

Word of God

The incarnate Word of God is the Christ. One of It's unlimited essences is as the manifested Absolute in the world of form. Its high level of knowing and being is called Christ Consciousness, which is available to all of us at the level of Spirit. (B)

The symbolic imagery of God speaking illustrates the metaphysical Truth that the Word, or Logos, is the potentializing aspect of God. It is the cosmic beingness which underwrites all manifestation. It is the Eternal Isness which forms Itself into light, sound, vibration, and energy. (B)

Work

Work is as much about daily meaning as it is about daily bread. (C)

All work, employment, and opportunities come through us, not to us. (C)

Some human souls experience a cacophony of jobs and occupations. Others graft themselves onto one line of work. Both routes are spiritual practices. Growth comes when there is congruence between who we are and what we do for a living. For some, work itself becomes a sort of morphine. For many, the asphyxia of suffocating work strangles their creativity and steals their health and happiness. Both routes mirror our spiritual unfoldment. Both hint at our alignment with Spirit. However, our chief occupation is burning off the dross of error and becoming consciously one with our Christ Nature. (B)

World

The physical world we know is our collective whirled consciousness spun on the axis of our imaginations. (B)

Metaphysically, the 'world' stands for our Adamic (sense) consciousness. (B)

World of Appearances

"Now you see it — now you don't!" These are famous words for magicians. The truth is we need to become "Spiritual Magicians!" We want to be able to call on our Truth Principles, look at the world of appearances and be able to say, "Now you see it, now you don't!" — to be able to look at negativity, or resentment, or anger, or fear, and be able to say, "Now you see it, now you don't!" — to make the challenging situations in our life disappear, and stand in the Truth of who we really are. (C)

It may look like things are not going well, or people are against you, or you have a black cloud over your head! But it is just appearance. Remember — we know (from our Power of Faith) that immutable Truth Principles are operating, and we live from that knowing. At the level of Spirit, all is well — and we live there, knowing we can transcend any appearance that seems otherwise. (C)

World Peace

My hope is that the horrors of war, and hunger, and disease will be replaced by the sounds of laughter, and the warmth of handshakes and hugs, and the reciprocity of goodwill. That will happen when the 'world' (our human consciousness) finds the peace (conscious alignment with the Christ Presence within) which passes all misunderstanding. (B)

Worship

I don't believe Spirit is particularly interested in our worship as much as It is in our Christship. By that I mean Spirit's desire is for us to become one with the Perfect Idea of God expressed as us. That Perfect Idea is the Christ which is God in physicality. If there's any 'worship' in the equation at all, it's the 'shaping of our worth" as spiritual beings having a human experience. That 'shaping' is up to us. It comes from pruning the parts of us that are pockets of error and replacing them with centers of Truth. (B)

Worthiness

What if you allowed yourself to declare your worthiness? What if you allowed yourself to claim what brings you the greatest joy? What if you affirmed that you deserve to earn the money you need to live the lifestyle you enjoy? What if you proclaimed your right to explore options? By boldly declaring your worthiness, you can open the pathway for your inner guidance to bring you incredible Divine Ideas which will move you to unbelievable opportunities. (C)

Negative self-talk is blasphemy. We are spiritual beings who have chosen a human experience. We are divine at our core. When we speak negatively about ourselves, we are misrepresenting who we really are. (B)

We should not judge our self worth by our net worth, because this kind of thinking steals our sense of worthiness and contentment. Instead, we must build our prosperity consciousness, realizing that God is the Source of our supply and that Truth and error cannot occupy the same place at the same time. (C)

There is something that is yours and yours alone to do — and NO ONE else in the whole world can do it the way you do it! But here's the deal: you must do it! (C)

Love yourself enough to conduct Personal Positive Pep Rallies. Affirm positive, loving, complimentary things about yourself. Seriously, do you realize how often people repeat negative, self-deprecating things about themselves? What we say, what we affirm about ourselves is imbedded in our consciousness. (C)

X-Factor

The capital X represents the first letter in the Greek word for Christ (Chi), and has been used as far back as Christianity itself as an abbreviation for Christ (hence, the derivation of Xmas — not demeaning to Christianity at all, but actually keeping Christ in Christmas!). When you live life from your highest, most elevated Christ Consciousness, you are exhibiting the True X-Factor! (C)

Yoke

Matthew 11:29 (NRSV) says: "Take my yoke upon you…and you will find rest." From a metaphysical perspective Matthew 11:29 says: "The more we discipline ourselves to follow Truth principles (take up the yoke), the more freedom from error and from the consequences of error we will have in actualizing our good (find rest)." (B)

Zeal

Bookend your day with zealous time in the Silence for prayer and meditation. Take time to ensure you are always prayed-up every morning and every evening, ready to go, always connected and aware of your Oneness with Spirit. By bookending your day, you are prayed up and ready to greet the day with Zeal, and in the right frame of mind to end the day with enthusiastic appreciation. Bookending your day with time at Headquarters (the Kingdom of Heaven within) puts your zealousness in the right perspective. (C)

One of our favorite quotes from Charles Fillmore is: *"I fairly sizzle with zeal and enthusiasm and I spring forth with a mighty faith to do the things that need to be done by me!"* What's amazing is he wrote this statement when he was 94 years old. (C)

Credits:

Book Cover and interior design: Cher Holton
Artwork/Photography:
© 2012 www.clipart.com: Pages 8, 19, 37, 50, 55, 61, 63, 68, 70, 78, 106, 118, 129, 130, 142, 163, 177, 180

p. 4 (© Kriss Szkuelatowski | stock.xchng)
p.14 (© D. Lockeretz | stock.xchng)
p. 25 (© lusi | stock.xchng)
p. 29 (© Iqoncept | Dreamstime.com)
p. 33 (© ? | Dreamstime.com)
p.43 (© John Byer| stock.xchng)
p. 59 (© Mushisushi | Dreamstime.com)
p. 70 (© Holton)
p. 74 (© nano-The Desktop Studio | iStockphoto.com)
p. 80 (© Holton)
p. 85 (© Lovliestdreams | Dreamstime.com)
p. 90 (stock.xchng)
p. 100 (© Holton)
p. 102 (© Holton)
p. 116 (© nevit | stock.xchng)
p. 122 (© Cheryl Empey | stock.xchng)
p. 141 (© Gabriella Fabbri | stock.xchng)
p. 148 (© Holton)
p. 152 (© Holton)
P. 156 (© Holton)
p. 169 (© AlexMax | iStockphoto.com)
p. 191-2 (© Focus Portraits)

Index

A

abundance 3, 21, 23, 42, 69, 83, 89, 94, 101, 106, 107, 122, 125
acceptance 4, 71, 86
Adam and Eve 5, 172
Advent wreath 34
affirmations 5, 6, 10, 21, 48, 110, 120, 127, 149, 156, 167
Akashic Records 7
angels 4, 8, 38, 71
Anti-Christ 9, 64
ascension 9
astral plane 10
astrology 10
at-One-ment 10, 11, 44, 52, 108, 145
attachments 11, 26, 44, 47, 98, 99, 131, 146, 170
attitude 15, 18, 32, 65, 70, 144, 147, 163
attraction 12, 127
authentic Self 1, 83, 119, 142
avatars 13
awareness 9, 11, 13, 17, 26, 34, 35, 38, 41, 51, 55, 60, 62, 65, 66, 78, 79, 84, 89, 93, 94, 107, 117, 118, 120, 122, 123, 136, 139, 141, 142, 145, 154, 157, 162, 172, 177

B

baptism 14
Beatitudes 15-19
belief 9, 18-20, 26, 28, 36, 41, 62, 66, 67, 76, 81, 87, 96, 98, 118, 123, 126, 134, 152, 159, 166, 172, 176
beliefs 13, 19, 20, 21, 29, 35, 51, 54, 60, 64, 85, 86, 95, 96, 99, 113, 117, 126, 144, 149, 151, 153, 162, 176
Bible 19, 21, 22, 50, 64, 113, 127, 130, 168, 174, 177, 178
blessings 23, 70
bliss 24, 138
blood 24, 39, 59, 75, 113, 130, 133, 172
body 25, 27, 40, 50, 54, 70, 73, 74, 75, 82, 96, 135, 139
born again 25, 26
brain 65, 67, 70, 80, 110, 133, 153
brotherhood 26
Buddha 30, 32, 158, 161
burning bush 26

C

cause and effect 27, 92
cellular theology 27
chakras 31, 77, 130, 178
challenges 41, 121, 149, 161
chemicalization 28, 64
choice 10, 25, 27, 29, 30, 69, 76, 91, 92, 94, 98, 109, 116, 121, 131, 139, 154, 170, 186
choices 21, 29, 30, 49, 54, 68, 79, 95, 96, 139, 140, 153, 154, 176, 178, 188
Christ 1, 2, 4, 9, 10, 11, 13, 15, 17, 20, 24, 30, 31, 32, 33, 34, 36, 40, 41, 43, 46, 47, 49, 50, 51, 52, 62, 64, 66, 68, 69, 72, 73, 74, 76, 77, 79, 80, 81, 82, 83, 84, 86, 87, 88, 89, 90, 92, 93, 95, 96, 97, 101, 107, 108, 109, 111, 112, 113, 115, 116, 119, 120, 121, 123, 124, 127, 128, 130, 134, 135, 136, 137, 139, 140, 141, 142, 143, 145, 146, 147, 152, 154, 155, 160, 161, 166, 169, 173, 175, 177, 179, 181
Christ Principle 34, 113
Christianity 32, 77, 82, 133
Christmas 33, 34, 106
coma consciousness 34, 35, 38, 143, 177
comfort 1, 15, 68, 90
comparative religions 35
consciousness 62
cosmic 2x4 36, 37
Cosmic Christ 36, 89, 113
cosmic net 37, 38
cosmology 38, 141
creativity 7, 52, 179
cross 22, 38, 39, 52, 53, 139
crucifixion 39, 50

D

dance 135, 152, 154
death/transition 40

denials 6, 10, 40, 41, 50, 149, 156, 167
denominations 41
diddlysquat order 43, 44
dis-ease 24, 41, 74, 75
discernment 32, 54, 139, 150
Divine 1, 3, 11, 13, 15, 16, 17, 18, 20, 23, 26, 31, 32, 34, 38, 39, 42, 43, 44, 45, 50, 60, 65, 69, 79, 80, 86, 88, 94, 96, 98, 104, 106, 113, 116, 123, 126, 132, 135, 137, 138, 140, 141, 147, 158, 175, 177, 178, 181
Divine Guidance 42
Divine Ideas 13, 17, 18, 23, 32, 42, 104, 106, 126, 181
Divine Order 13, 43, 44, 132
divinity 16, 17, 18, 30, 33, 35, 42, 60, 73, 78, 79, 81, 83, 88, 92, 101, 114, 115, 116, 117, 140, 144, 145, 148, 150, 157, 161, 165, 168, 173
dogma 2, 7, 20, 32, 45, 46, 64, 84, 86, 87, 105, 113, 117
dominion 35, 46
doubt 40, 45, 47, 53, 84, 104, 106, 110, 119, 120, 121, 149, 159, 177
Doubting Thomas Effect 47

E

each-consecutive-moment-of-now 13, 49, 124
Easter 39, 49, 50, 70
echo power 162
ego 21, 28, 31, 34, 49, 51, 56, 58, 61, 74, 81, 87, 93, 115, 121, 140, 143, 162, 175
embedded theology 51
enlightenment 1, 26, 27, 30, 32, 52, 65, 77, 82, 115, 119, 121, 132, 134, 136, 140, 144, 145
entrainment 52, 166
error thinking 53, 60, 86, 96, 110, 136, 145, 156
eternal Life 55, 77, 89
evil 18, 55, 164
evolution 56, 115
experience 56

F

Facebook 26
failures 55, 109
faith 1, 2, 3, 21, 35, 36, 41, 45, 51, 57, 58, 76, 78, 85, 86, 98, 107, 115, 123, 132, 133, 134, 141, 147, 150, 155, 164, 166, 167, 169, 170, 175, 177, 180, 183
false prophets 4, 59
fasting 60
fate 60, 92
fear 2, 34, 40, 41, 51, 53, 56, 59, 60, 61, 62, 74, 80, 104, 109, 119, 123, 125, 133, 139, 145, 146, 149, 154, 155, 159, 167, 175, 180
finances 3
First Coming 62
fish 37, 46, 49
forgiveness 38, 62, 63, 73, 121, 157, 168, 173, 177
four horsemen 64
future 7, 30, 49, 71, 88, 107, 133, 174

G

Garden of Eden 65
Genesis 46, 65, 96, 130, 171
Giving 23, 35, 47, 49, 63, 65, 66, 70, 94, 99, 110, 118, 120, 125, 127, 163, 168, 170
God 2, 10, 13, 17, 19, 26, 31, 32, 33, 34, 36, 44, 46, 50, 51, 52, 58, 60, 61, 62, 65, 66, 67, 68, 78, 79, 81, 84, 85, 86, 87, 88, 89, 91, 93, 94, 95, 96, 98, 103, 107, 111, 112, 117, 119, 120, 122, 123, 128, 130, 132, 133, 138, 140, 141, 145, 148, 149, 150, 151, 155, 158, 159, 161, 165, 166, 167, 171, 179, 181, 182
Golden Buddha 30
good Samaritan 68
grace 11, 65, 68, 69, 76, 115, 126, 146
gratitude 69, 70, 71, 161
great villain 22
greater good 3, 58, 127
guilt 2, 34, 39, 80, 102, 123, 125, 139, 145, 159

H

habits 18, 28, 38, 53, 104, 112, 151, 162, 170, 176
happiness 24, 31, 32, 36, 44, 52, 55, 72, 83, 90, 98, 100, 101, 106, 125, 126, 179
harmony 24, 72, 73, 90, 98, 176
healing 21, 31, 42, 73, 121, 146, 169
health 3, 27, 31, 41, 52, 83, 88, 92, 100, 104, 106, 121, 125, 133, 153, 179
Heaven 7, 15, 17, 18, 75, 76, 87, 92, 93, 96, 99, 111, 120, 132, 144, 183
Hell 75, 76, 77, 87
Holy City 77
Holy Spirit 68, 77, 136, 168
hope 2, 23, 30, 52, 65, 72, 78, 112, 132, 181, 186
humankind 1, 2, 10, 11, 22, 31, 41, 52, 61, 67, 78, 88, 96, 113, 119, 130, 132, 157, 158, 169, 177

I

I Thessalonians 16 161
identity 79, 113, 143
illness 4, 5, 37, 41, 63, 68. 72, 74, 75, 120, 160, 167, 176
illusion 14, 52, 54, 59, 60, 80, 81, 87, 89, 105, 113, 121, 126, 131, 139, 146, 159
immaculate conception 81
immortality 81, 119
incarnation 10, 47, 81, 82, 105, 131
inconvenient Truth 82
indwelling Spirit 83
inner expansion 48
intelligent design 84
intention 2, 3, 11, 21, 29, 69, 84, 85, 139, 170, 173
interfaith tradition 85
irreconcilable differences 86, 112, 168

J

jalopied Spirituality 87
Jerusalem effect 87
Jesus 1, 5, 6, 15, 20, 22, 24, 30, 34, 37, 40, 46, 49, 50, 52, 55, 60, 62, 77, 84, 86, 87, 88, 89, 93, 97, 99, 101, 113, 115, 116, 125, 130, 139, 144, 146, 149, 152, 158, 160, 164, 166, 175, 186
John 3:16 89
John 8:12 89
John 10:10 160
John 14:14 89
joy 23, 27, 34, 42, 55, 60, 65, 70, 90, 93, 120, 126, 138, 139, 154, 159, 181
Judgment Day 91

K

karma 60, 92
kindness 16, 68, 70, 92
Kingdom of Heaven 7, 15, 17, 18, 92, 93, 120, 183
Kundalini 31, 77, 93, 136

L

lack consciousness 94
life 4, 7, 3, 4, 6, 7, 9, 15, 21, 23, 28, 29, 40, 45, 46, 48, 50, 55, 57, 59, 64, 68, 71, 72, 73, 77, 79, 85, 88, 89, 90, 94, 95, 98, 104, 109, 110, 112, 116, 119, 120, 121, 122, 123, 126, 129, 136, 140, 144, 146, 149, 153, 156, 157, 158, 160, 165, 167, 171, 178, 180, 186, 188
light 8, 13, 23, 31, 35, 52, 57, 60, 67, 78, 83, 89, 95, 96, 117, 134, 157, 176, 179
literal interpretations 19, 86, 96, 97, 134
Lord's Supper 5, 97
love 7, 16, 23, 34, 44, 46, 62, 73, 81, 97, 98, 114, 121, 150, 152, 155, 165, 173, 175, 177, 182, 186
Luke 18:18, 20-24 99

M

magi 33
manifest 3, 6, 13, 21, 23, 44, 66, 67, 68, 77, 89, 101, 104, 119, 126, 127, 161, 165
manifestation 3, 21, 103, 179
maskunfusion 80
materialism 72, 100
Matthew 13:12 101
meditation 5, 20, 21, 53, 73, 101, 102,

104, 110, 116, 120, 127, 150, 152, 154, 156, 157, 160, 183
meek 15, 16
mental kudzu 103
metaphysical 18, 22, 32, 38, 39, 46, 51, 68, 86, 89, 99, 102, 103, 105, 116, 128, 136, 137, 142, 147, 149, 150, 166, 169, 175, 177, 179, 183, 186, 188
metaphysical malpractice 102, 103
metaphysics 7, 17, 100, 103, 186, 188
millstones 10, 43, 159
mind action 21, 95, 104, 105, 159
mind-critters 54
miracles 105
mistranslation 16, 17, 18, 50, 171
money 11, 32, 41, 59, 65, 70, 79, 94, 99, 100, 106, 107, 125, 167, 176, 181
monkey mind 102
Mt. Sinai 107
Multiverse 36, 131, 164, 171
mysticism 107

N

namaste 109
negative thinking 109, 159, 160
neuro-theology 110, 140
neurons 65, 104, 105, 153

O

obstacles 118
Omni 111
one reality 38, 67, 85
oneness 9, 34, 38, 40, 43, 51, 60, 62, 67, 76, 78, 84, 86, 98, 108, 109, 111, 112, 117, 123, 136, 139, 141, 154, 155, 159, 172, 175, 178, 183
Only-Begotten Son 113
optical delusions 113, 114
original sin 114

P

pain 54, 62, 82, 115, 129
Palm Sunday 115, 116
peace 6, 8, 13, 17, 23, 26, 27, 34, 52, 62, 68, 71, 78, 82, 83, 86, 87, 90, 93, 98, 106, 112, 115, 116, 117, 120, 122, 123, 126, 135, 138, 139, 160, 173, 175, 176, 181
pediatric theology 117
Pentecost 117
perception 13, 61, 66
personality 22, 52, 119, 142, 143, 146, 172, 177, 186
philosopher's stone 119
Pontius Pilate 22, 49, 113
practicing the Presence 22, 120
prayer 10, 20, 21, 38, 48, 53, 73, 74, 86, 93, 101, 104, 110, 120, 122, 123, 124, 127, 138, 150, 152, 156, 157, 160, 183
prosperity 12, 13, 21, 23, 36, 44, 71, 93, 94, 106, 107, 122, 124, 125, 126, 127, 150, 151, 182, 186
Proverbs 23:7 128
Proverbs 6:6 127
Proverbs 9:1 178
Psalm 23 136
pyramids 31, 165

Q

quantum 27, 28, 36, 38, 67, 82, 84, 140, 141, 164, 171
quantum turbulence 28
questions 2, 129, 163, 188

R

rainbow 31, 119, 130
reincarnation 131
relationships 3, 37, 62, 106, 176
religion 2, 45, 59, 84, 85, 86, 105, 108, 112, 132, 133, 134, 140
religious victrolas 134
rescuing hug 73
rest 52, 74, 123, 125, 129, 134, 135, 138, 151, 183
resurrection 60, 135
Revelation 14:22 136
Revelation 21:21b 136
righteousness 136
ritual 14, 123, 137
Romans 8:28 137

S

sabbath 138, 168
sacred writings 22, 134
sacrifice 139
salvation 139
satan 140
science 1, 38, 75, 84, 86, 112, 140, 141, 186, 188
Scrooge-ology 33
Second Coming 141, 142
self 142
self worth 107, 182
self-knowledge 143
sense consciousness 68, 93, 143, 146, 166
separation 5, 9, 14, 26, 36, 41, 52, 59, 60, 62, 76, 81, 84, 86, 89, 96, 105, 111, 112, 115, 119, 121, 123, 131, 134, 136, 139, 146, 159, 164, 166, 172, 178
Sermon on the Mount 144
serpent 77, 144
service 10, 17, 70, 117, 144, 145, 150, 188
shepherds 33
SHOOT 151
Silence 42, 53, 101, 102, 120, 122, 173, 183
sin 39, 114, 145, 168
skin school 38, 40, 55, 78, 96, 131, 146
somatic spacesuit 25
Son of Man 77, 146
Song of Solomon, 2:15 147
Speaking in Tongues 147
Spirit 4, 8, 9, 14, 15, 24, 25, 26, 27, 34, 35, 38, 42, 43, 44, 49, 50, 51, 52, 55, 56, 58, 59, 60, 62, 65, 66, 68, 69, 73, 76, 77, 81, 82, 83, 87, 94, 97, 98, 105, 106, 108, 111, 112, 115, 117, 119, 120, 121, 123, 126, 131, 135, 136, 138, 142, 147, 148, 149, 155, 161, 164, 168, 172, 175, 177, 179, 180, 181, 183
spiritual Alka Seltzer 28
spiritual apps 148
spiritual cataracts 149, 150
spiritual DNA 42, 113
spiritual Drano 159
spiritual echo-nomics 5, 150

spiritual economics 150
spiritual growth 2, 6, 20, 21, 28, 32, 38, 39, 47, 48, 50, 54, 57, 58, 63, 64, 76, 82, 95, 99, 101, 104, 110, 115, 120, 131, 134, 137, 150, 151, 152, 156, 159, 166, 169, 173
spiritual hydration 154
spiritual journey 2, 59, 118, 156
spiritual obstetrics 25, 154
spiritual orthopedics 155
spiritual practice 17, 60, 93, 102, 119, 125, 134, 149, 154, 155
spiritual purpose 157
spiritual teachers 158
spiritual tweets 6, 149, 153
spirituality 2, 11, 18, 38, 47, 51, 54, 68, 85, 86, 87, 110, 134, 138, 139, 141, 154, 155, 163, 169, 186, 188
Still Small Voice 117, 138, 158
struggle 109, 159
subconscious 3, 28, 158
suffering 18, 39, 72, 121, 130, 159, 160
superconscious 11, 24
Superman Christ 160

T

texting 144, 148, 149
Thanksliving 69, 161
The Fall 4, 59
theology 6, 1, 18, 22, 27, 38, 45, 46, 47, 48, 51, 59, 63, 79, 84, 85, 96, 110, 117, 123, 132, 133, 140
Third Coming 161, 177
thought power 161
tithing 163
transcendence 164
tree of knowledge 164
tree of life 165
Trinity 140, 165
Truth 2, 4, 5, 6, 9, 11, 12, 13, 15, 16, 18, 20, 24, 26, 27, 34, 36, 38, 41, 45, 47, 51, 52, 53, 56, 57, 59, 61, 79, 82, 84, 85, 86, 88, 94, 98, 99, 101, 102, 105, 106, 113, 114, 115, 116, 118, 121, 126, 132, 141, 146, 147, 148, 149, 150, 151, 153, 155,

157, 162, 163, 166, 167, 168, 173, 174, 177, 179, 180, 181, 182, 183, 186, 188
Truth Principles 5, 11, 16, 34, 36, 47, 57, 105, 106, 121, 150, 151, 153, 157, 162, 167, 177, 180, 183, 186

U

unforgivable sin 168
unity 2, 41, 50, 67, 101, 133, 134, 137, 168, 169
universal substance 66, 170, 171
universality 67, 131, 170
universe 5, 7, 10, 21, 27, 38, 67, 73, 81, 126, 141, 164, 171, 172
unquiet city 172

V

violence 26, 172, 173
virgin birth 173
vow 173

W

"wait" lifting 174
walking on water 97, 174, 175
walking the talk 174
war 4, 26, 64, 175, 181
wealth 11, 31, 119, 125, 170, 176
white light 176
wholeness 27, 41, 56, 68, 73, 74, 145, 177
widowhood 177
winged globe 177
wisdom 32, 38, 68, 86, 87, 89, 97, 120, 127, 128, 146, 155, 158, 177, 178
work 2, 3, 5, 8, 10, 11, 17, 21, 26, 29, 39, 41, 42, 43, 44, 48, 79, 90, 105, 115, 131, 137, 151, 160, 161, 177, 179, 186, 187
world 180
world of appearances 180
worship 35, 74, 117, 143, 158, 181
worthiness 181, 182

X

X Factor 182

Y

yoke 183

Z

zeal 183

About the Authors:

Combine a flair for the dramatic, a deep understanding of metaphysics combined with the teachings of Jesus, and a zest for ministry, and you have defined the dynamic duo who co-authored this book. This exciting couple brings their love for Truth Principles to everything they do, and thrives on inviting people to walk the spiritual path on practical feet.

Revs. Bil and Cher Holton bring quite a background of business experience to their spiritual work. Together they founded The Holton Consulting Group, Inc. in 1982, and have worked with clients in the U.S., Canada, Germany, England, and South America, with a mission of leading, guiding, and inspiring people and organizations to live productively and joyfully at the speed of life ... one choice at a time.

As a subsidiary of their consulting firm, the Holtons created two publishing enterprises: Liberty Publishing Group (focusing on professional and personal publications) and Prosperity Publishing House (for spiritual material). They have published over 50 titles, including *The New Metaphysical Versions of Matthew, Mark, Luke, and John* (the first ever verse-by-verse metaphysical interpretation of the four Gospels) and *The Metaphysical New Testament, Volumes I and II.*

Rev. Dr. Bil Holton has been writing, speaking, coaching, and publishing for over 30 years. Bil has a solid reputation for his strength of character, engaging personality, and strong work ethic. His extraordinary metaphysical teachings and his ability to bring spiritual Truths into clarity by combining science and spirituality put him in high demand as a teacher and spiritual coach. When he isn't involved in neuroscience research, studies in quantum physics, and metaphysical writing, Bil enjoys golf, travel, ballroom dancing, jigsaw puzzles, the theatre, and landscaping.

**Rev. Dr. Cher Holton** claims her name is an acronym for her personal mission: Creating Hope, Enthusiasm, and Results ... and she brings her zest for living and her practical applications of Truth principles to everything she does. Her background includes being a "Preacher's Kid," a Certified Speaking Professional, and a Certified Management Consultant, which make her a much sought after facilitator, speaker, and coach. When she isn't involved in spiritual study and professional speaking, Cher enjoys a good mystery novel, crossword and logic puzzles, ballroom dancing, the theatre and performing arts, travel, and print matter design work.

On a personal note *(more straight talk about Bil and Cher)*:

Bil and Cher take what they call "Indiana Jones Experiences" including white-water rafting, sky-diving, helicopter fly-bys and even fire walking to push their risk-taking envelopes. But one of their most exciting adventures led them into the world of ballroom dancing, and they are amateur student couple champions in several ballroom dance categories. They even have a ballroom dance floor in their home!

The Holtons have three grandchildren who live close to them, and provide Bil and Cher many opportunities to bond with them ... and then give them back to their parents! (That's what grandparents do — right?)

A Sampling of Other Books by the Holtons:

By Rev. Dr. Bil Holton:
The Gospel of Matthew, New Metaphysical Version
The Gospel of Mark, New Metaphysical Version
The Gospel of Luke, New Metaphysical Version
The Gospel of John, New Metaphysical Version
The Dance Between Science and Spirituality
Get Over It! The Truth About What You Know That Just Ain't So! (co-authored with Paul Hasselbeck)
Get Over These, Too! More Truth About What You Know That Just Ain't So! (Co-authored with Paul Hasselbeck)

By Rev. Dr. Cher Holton:
Living at the Speed of Life: Staying in Control in a World Gone Bonkers!
PowerUP: The Twelve Powers Revisited as Accelerated Abilities (co-authored with Paul Hasselbeck)
Applying Heart-Centered Metaphysics: A Workbook to Bring Metaphysics To Life in Your Life (co-authored with Paul Hasselbeck)

Co-Authored by Revs. Drs. Bil & Cher Holton:
The Manager's Short Course to a Long Career
Crackerjack Choices: 200 of the Best Choices You Will Ever Make
From Ballroom to Bottom Line ... in business and in life
Business Prayers for Millennium Managers
SUPPOSE . . . Questions to Turbo-Charge Your Business and Your Life

They also have many digital books available in a variety of formats through Smashwords.com/profile/view/bilholton

To order books or invite the Holtons to speak at your organization, spiritual center, or association, contact them at:
service@TheMetaphysicalWebsite.com or info@HoltonConsulting.com

We invite you to visit their cutting-edge website, read their blog, and sign up for their newsletter at:
www.TheMetaphysicalWebsite.com